SOUTHERN PLACES

A Classic Collection of
WORDS & IMAGES

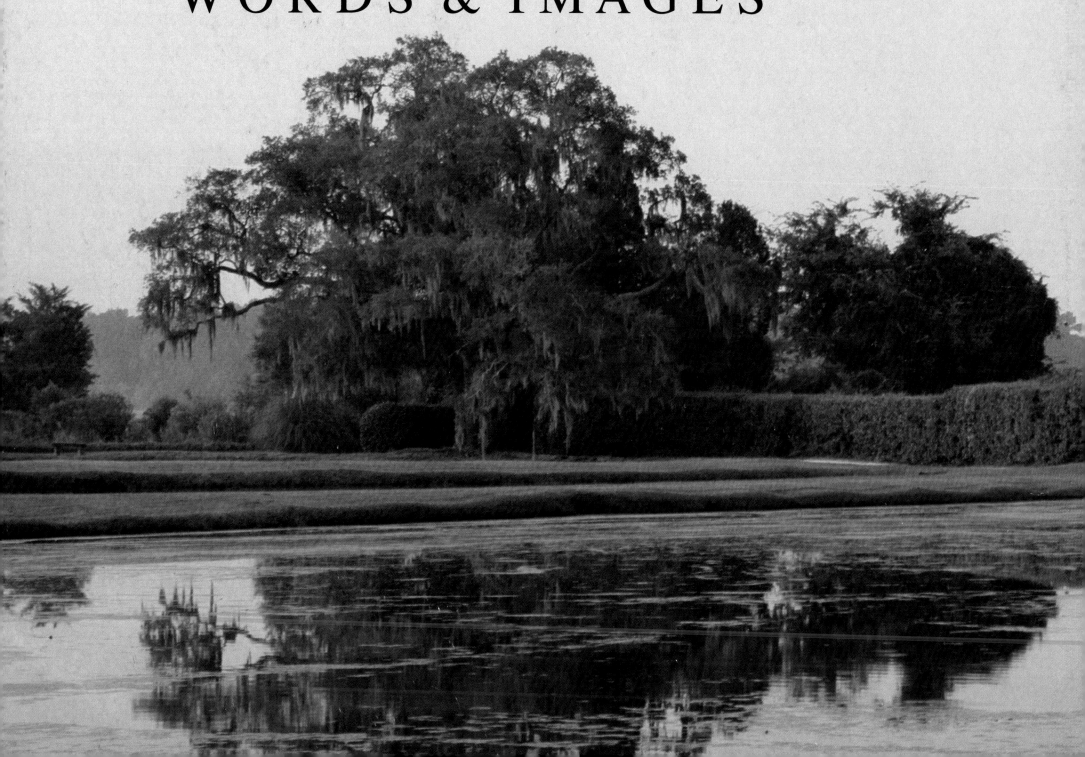

©1990 by Oxmoor House, Inc.
Book Division of Southern Progress Corporation
P.O. Box 2463, Birmingham, Alabama 35201

Library of Congress Number: 90-062263
ISBN: 0-8487-1010-X
Manufactured in the United States of America

First Edition

Executive Editor: Nancy J. Fitzpatrick
Production Manager: Jerry Higdon
Associate Production Manager: Rick Litton
Art Director: Bob Nance

SOUTHERN PLACES
originated with Philip Morris,
Executive Editor, SOUTHERN LIVING®

Editor: Rebecca Brennan
Senior Designer: Cynthia Rose Cooper
Production Assistant: Theresa L. Beste
Editorial Assistant: Lelia Gray Neil

Land of the South, © Oxmoor House, served as a vital
reference in the writing of "One Place, Many Places."

Contents

Introduction

The old neighborhood. A college quadrangle. A favorite resort or much-visited historic town. The resounding public building or a quiet garden. These are among the many places the South holds dear. They are the focus, in photographs and words, of *Southern Places*.

The region gathers its larger sense of place as much from social custom and language and shared history as it does from physical places. This book concentrates on the latter, though woven through are intangibles. It is the landscape, the town, the battlefield, the church that are pictured and discussed. What took place in these places—the layers of shared and personal experience—are implicit.

The selection is simply that: a selection. This is not an encyclopedia of Southern locale. These photographs represent a distillation from those published in the pages of *Southern Living* over the years. The essays and descriptions were written by editors of the magazine. Places presented are organized into categories, but with the understanding that very many places defy neat classification. A college campus is also a social and a public place. A stretch of coastline makes a place of itself but also a place of sport or recreation. At their most memorable, the places Southerners love carry layers of meaning.

Many of the places are singular. Others represent types of places found across the region. And a preponderance are historic. This is not merely

nostalgia, though that is what good places often deservedly elicit. Older places have accumulated more meaning, but they also very often are more tied to a specific setting or are simply more humane in scale or character—and thereby more engaging—than new places. And so follows a motive behind this collection of Southern Places: that there is a difference between those landscapes and buildings and urban districts in the South that contribute a sense of place and those that do not. The best lessons for making places people can love are found in those places that people already do. They are fondly portrayed on these pages, at least in part on the hope they might inspire others.

Philip Morris

*I*n the Colonial period, Virginia was the largest and most influential of the colonies, developing a leadership role that would carry through the early decades of the new nation. Traces of the Colonial period are still much in evidence in Virginia and Maryland, both in the architecture and layout of towns and in such celebratory events as this annual parade in Alexandria, Virginia. Until the early nineteenth century, population was concentrated on the South's eastern seaboard.

*B*elow the Grand Strand of wide beach extending along the northern half of the South Carolina coast, the Sea Islands zone begins. A virtual stew of islands, bays, marshes, seaside forests, and tide-influenced rivers, it reaches along the South Carolina and Georgia coasts and embraces such celebrated places as Charleston and Beaufort, South Carolina; Hilton Head Island; Savannah, Georgia; St. Simons and Jekyll islands. Destruction from the Civil War and hurricanes, plus competition from new rice-growing areas, put an end to the rice culture.

*N*orth Carolina's Outer Banks, the longest natural feature of its kind in the world, makes an uneasy peace with Atlantic Ocean storms and currents. As a result, there was sparse settlement, making a break in coastal character. It has always been a place apart, tied to the sea more than the land. Much of the most fragile barrier island environment is now protected as the Cape Hatteras and Cape Lookout National Seashores. Fishing remains a vital way of life.

*T*he Piedmont, or "foot of the mountains," is a rolling inland plain that extends from the fall line, marking the boundary with the coastal plain to the Blue Ridge and Appalachian mountain ranges. These lands had red clay, generally harder for growing crops, so settlement came more slowly. The Virginia Piedmont, shown here, was culturally an extension of the Virginia Tidewater, in contrast to a different character found in the Carolinas Piedmont farther south.

A *small, independent farmer class settled the North Carolina and South Carolina Piedmont beginning in the mid-eighteenth century. These were predominantly Scotch-Irish and German stock moving down the Shenandoah Valley road. Even though the soils were not ideal and often quickly exhausted, tobacco and other cash crops generated a culture quite different from the plantation traditions to the east. The short, rapidly flowing rivers that cut perpendicularly across the Piedmont toward the coast were first a disadvantage to settlement, but later they powered the mills that began to transform this band of territory into an industrial and urban region, a characteristic that continues today.*

*T*he Blue Ridge Mountains, extending in a band running south and west through Maryland, Virginia, North Carolina, South Carolina, Tennessee, and northern Georgia, include a series of subunits with their own names, such as the Great Smoky Mountains. In its southern sweep, the Blue Ridge has forty-six peaks above six thousand feet elevation. These are older mountains, originally the continent's Atlantic shoreline, and they are notably green, supporting a rich array of plant materials in widely varied microclimates. The Great Smoky Mountains alone contain more than 130 tree species, greater than the number found in all of Western Europe. Cades Cove, Tennessee, seen in this view, is a historic agricultural valley nestled at the foot of the mountains, now managed by the National Park Service as part of the Great Smoky Mountains National Park.

*T*he Shenandoah Valley of Virginia is part of the great Valley and Ridge system that extends from Pennsylvania to Alabama parallel and just west of the Blue Ridge. The strong ridges define the edges of valleys, the widest being the Shenandoah. Limestone-based soils in the valley made it very fertile, and early settlers from the North brought their agricultural and cultural inclinations with them. Wheat, a variety of grains, cattle, and horses were raised. There was virtually no cotton, and no slaves were used in this region.

*L*ocated at the northern end of the Shenandoah Valley, Winchester, Virginia, was established in 1774 and served as an important market town for the valley and a supply point for westward-bound pioneers. The town's historic fabric is largely intact and restored.

Classic Deep South cotton country once predominated in a zone called the Eastern Gulf Coastal Plain, which extends from southwest Georgia and the Florida Panhandle west through Alabama, most of Mississippi, and up into western Tennessee. Though cotton has long since ended its reign, traces of the past remain in far-flung plantation houses and a rural economy where pastures are as prevalent as cultivated fields. Though this area is known as the Old South, it was actually a newly settled country in the decades just before the Civil War. Alabama's population, for example, was only about nine thousand in 1810 but had jumped to nearly one million by 1860. Today the Black Belt, named for its rich soil, provides a pleasant small-town life for some, like these children riding on the fringes of Livingston, Alabama. However, deep poverty pervades much of its rural black population, where agricultural work has all but disappeared.

The fate of geologic formations created great differences in a subregion located west of the Valley and Ridge and north of the Eastern Gulf Coastal Plain. The Appalachian Plateau's sandstone and shale eroded into rugged country with poor soils, though with significant coal beneath. In contrast, limestone formations that gave way to the Lexington (Kentucky) Plain and the Nashville (Tennessee) Basin produced land that was highly productive and attracted a settlement that thrived. This history is highly visible today in the prosperous city of Lexington, with its world-famous horse farms.

*T*he Florida peninsula is one of the most clearly defined and unusual regions of the South. With a low shelf of rock as its base, the peninsula has moderate elevation change ranging from zero to three hundred feet above sea level. There are more than nine thousand miles of coastline in Florida, with great diversity of environment: barrier islands and mainland beaches, swamps and marshes, coral reefs, mangrove forests, and many other natural variations. The climate ranges from temperate to tropical, moderated by coastal breezes. Among the string of islands along the Gulf Coast near Fort Myers is Captiva Island, where strict growth management has helped preserve its natural amenities. Florida was once thinly populated, but for several decades it has been growing at a rate several hundred percent greater than the national average.

Resort development has played an important role in Florida growth and life since the first railroads were extended across and down the peninsula in the early 1900s. The great concentration of Art Deco resort architecture built at Miami Beach earlier in this century is now part of a protected historic district.

The Mississippi Valley and Delta, shaped by an ever-changing river and the diverse cultures that found it attractive, forms a fertile zone that divides the eastern part of the South from the western. One of its most distinctive cultural traditions is that of the French-speaking Acadians who settled in the southern part of Louisiana west of Baton Rouge, and who make a living from the bayous.

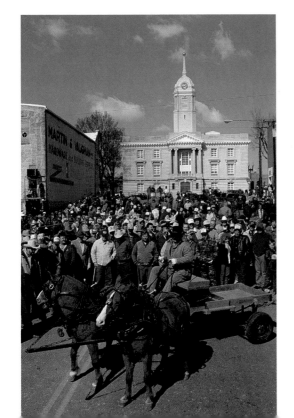

At Columbia, Tennessee, south of Nashville, the traditional rural trade role of the city centered in a productive farming area is celebrated each year with Mule Day. The city was also home to James K. Polk, who was elected eleventh president of the United States in 1844 during a period of rapid westward expansion.

The Ozark and Ouachita Uplands which extend through northwestern Arkansas and parts of eastern Oklahoma were created by a prehistoric collision of continental plates. Though not as high or extensive as the Blue Ridge Mountains, the topography can be very dramatic, especially along rivers that have cut through rock over eons to form stunning bluffs.

The largest and most populous of the Southern subregions is called the West Gulf Coastal Plain, covering much of western Louisiana, portions of Arkansas and southern Oklahoma, and a vast stretch of east, central, and south Texas. Most settlers came from the lower South. Others came to central Texas from the upper South, to the Hill Country from German immigrants who landed on the Gulf Coast, and to south Texas from Mexican natives. The photograph shows the Huntsville, Texas, home of Sam Houston, who crossed into Texas in 1832 to become an early leader and organizer of the state.

Located on the Balcones Escarpment where the coastal plain meets the Hill Country, Austin, Texas, marks the point of transition from the warm and humid Gulf zone to the higher, drier elevations reaching north and west through the vast state it serves as capital. A once erratic flow of the Colorado River through Austin and the Hill Country has been tamed to make a series of lakes bounded by live oak-studded hills. Town Lake extends through the heart of the city.

Cactus growing on the Y & O Ranch near Kerrville, Texas, indicate clearly that this subregion is appropriately termed The Dry Margin in relation to the rest of the region.

The last major area opened to white settlement in the South was the more than eight million acres of Indian Territory purchased by the United States government and thrown open to homesteading. A large portion of this land was opened at noon, April 22, 1889, and by the end of the day the town of Guthrie, Oklahoma, which served as first state capital, counted ten thousand residents. Recent restoration has preserved many buildings constructed in Guthrie in the years immediately following settlement.

Bower Towns And Boom Cities

Traditionally tied to an agricultural region, Southern urban places were generally dispersed, not very dense and, though less dynamic than Northern counterparts, very often beautiful. More recent urbanization has spawned metropolitan areas with close contrasts of skyscrapers and garden suburbs.

What role towns and cities have played in shaping the South as a region has long been ignored or dismissed as unsubstantial. The region was distinguished by its rural character, as historical statistics make clear. By the beginning of the Civil War the South had less than 10 percent of its population living in cities, while the national urban percentage was twice that. In 1900, the differences were more pronounced: 18 percent urban in the South, 40 percent nationally, and more than 60 percent in the Northeast. What cities and towns? might come the question. And the response would be: Charleston, Annapolis, Williamsburg, Savannah, San Antonio, New Orleans—cities counted among the most distinctive in the nation. And, continuing the list with places evoking images and character, come Nashville, Richmond, Lexington, Austin, Winston-Salem, Sarasota, Aiken, Asheville, followed by the big, bright urban stars of the region's recent past: Dallas, Atlanta, Houston, Miami, and Washington, D.C.

Statistics, percentages, and historic research which indicate that the region had mostly marginal urbanization for most of its life, with cities and towns limited by dependence on staple crop rural economies, should not obscure the reality. There were cities and towns, of varying description, size, location, and geography, out there on the landscape, baking in summer heat or half-empty for long stretches while crops were being planted, some hardly visible for the trees and shrubs lining the streets, most hardly providing a minimum of urban service and life.

But, still, below that central Georgia hill, stretched out along broad streets lined with vigorous buildings leading down to the grand train station, this is Macon—a city. And though subject to vagaries of crops and weather and river moods, there stands on the bluff above the Mississippi another city named Memphis. Places at crossroads, at river fall lines, on harbors, tucked in agricultural valleys, hugging hillsides in the mountains; places with streets, courthouse squares, markets, churches, grand avenues, under-the-hill black quarters, campuses, hospitals; urban places for better or worse, for richer or poorer, wed to the region that contains them.

There was not anything as focused and imageable as the New England town in the Southern counterpart. From the beginning, the region developed uncentered, for the most part, scattered across the agricultural landscape. Towns, when they occurred, tended to be loosely organized, half-town, half-country in feeling. The real cities, at the earliest, developed around ports, and though few in number, they rivaled those farther north. Charleston was a world-city in its heyday. New Orleans, at the top of its pre-railroad-era cotton boom, had growth rates that promised to make it the largest city in the nation.

Rapid growth of the railroad as the new river of commerce, which began in earnest in the 1830s and 1840s, simultaneously limited growth of port cities along the Southern coast and initiated a whole new crescent of cities inland in an arc stretching through the valleys and Piedmont region of Virginia, North Carolina, and South Carolina, as well as along a network of developing towns and cities at strategic junctions all across the new map of rail lines. Some cities benefited from both historic water and new rail connections, but there were major urban concentrations blooming, at Roanoke, at Atlanta, at Birmingham, where rivers had never been a factor. It is ironic that this dislocation of economic force inland helped maintain the period place character of many Colonial-era Southern cities and towns. Had it not

been so, Charleston and Savannah might have long ago disappeared under the weight of a railroad-era boom.

Even with the wider network of urbanization that came from railroads, the relatively undynamic quality of Southern towns and cities (most were market towns for rural areas, not independent manufacturing-driven economies) kept the South from experiencing the denser, more compact city patterns found in the Northeast and the Northern industrial heartland. The fact is, when growth and prosperity came to a greater number of Southern cities after recovery from the Civil War, much of the new development came in the form of early suburban patterns. The loosely developed Southern town, commented on more for its bowers than its burg, was now paralleled by the city of stitched-together garden suburbs. As the proportion of Southern urban population increased to 28 percent in 1920, 34 percent in 1930, and on up to more than 50 percent in 1960, the traditional, highly imageable, tight urban development was not found except in certain older towns and in central districts. The row house was never the rule in Southern cities. The garden district starting a block from main street was repeated again and again.

There are many factors that have shaped towns and cities in the South. Sometimes there were visionary plans, but not often. Savannah, with its multiple squares and hierarchy of major and minor streets laid out by General James Oglethorpe and perpetuated through the nineteenth century by municipal control of land, is a remarkable exception. So is

Annapolis, organized in a baroque order of radiating streets and important public building vistas. Most often, Southern towns were established on grids, with sometimes a courthouse square at the center as focus. The grid was the new American rational model favored by Thomas Jefferson, and it made for easy land subdivision and speculation. The latter sometimes did produce interesting effects: competing grids, where rival land companies would lay out street grids on different orientation. A place such as downtown Montgomery, Alabama, takes on character from such conflict, as does downtown Dallas.

Geography has also been a force bringing character to many Southern urban settlements. Hills distort grids and create dramatic juxtapositions. Rivers define urban edges and centers, and bays order whole metropolitan zones. The Norfolk-Hampton Roads area in Virginia is a diverse mosaic structured around water. Jacksonville, Florida, has the broad St. Johns River sweeping through its heart and dramatic bridges making heroic crossings, with neighborhoods of every description from city center to idyllic residential compound oriented to this great, blue, open space. And even a young city like Birmingham, founded as an industrial new town only in 1871, developed in a linear form in response to powerful Appalachian ridges extending through its territory.

Architecture expressive of a particular period or locale also distinguishes many Southern cities and towns, ranging from Georgian or Federal accumulations in Eastern Seaboard states to Spanish

Colonial in selected Texas locations. The great and extended Greek and Roman Revival periods in the South set the civic tone for many towns, like Milledgeville in Georgia or Bath in North Carolina. The fullest realization of this antebellum town style remains, in at least the more wishful recesses of memory, as the pinnacle of urban civility in the region.

The truth is, however, that the places such as Alexandria, Virginia, or Charleston, South Carolina, or the Vieux Carré in New Orleans, where there is a whole and rounded town style realized in all its glory are, and always have been, the exception. Most American and Southern cities are layered from many periods and architectural styles, and the same periods and styles can be found in Louisville or Norfolk or Nashville, with local variations. These layers represent the period of growth rather than an indigenous style of building. There are, of course, particular Gulf Coast or other often subregional characteristics that come into play, so the same period layers will "feel" different even though they echo national trends.

While the most recent tendency toward urban sprawl may threaten to blur all Southern urban places into one anonymous nowhere, there remain embedded in the Southern landscape today many, many cities and towns of memorable character. The towns are easier to hold in the mind's eye whole, and even though they share patterns of development and periods of building they will usually have qualities as distinctive as a thumbprint. Railroad town. River town. Main Street town. Crossroads.

Cities, the larger they grow, are by nature more complex. Impressions are gained sequentially or sporadically, and the total image comes from many different aspects. The contemporary city has been described as a collage of parts stitched together, more or less well, by major transportation corridors. The skyline is often the most boasted about feature, though the more satisfying places within cities—the places residents and visitors prefer to spend time—are often older districts built in a period before the skyscraper when the scale was more intimate. The greater the selection of singular places a city offers, the richer its experience. These may be great plazas, lively waterfronts, boulevards of grand scope or sidewalks alive with people, landmark churches or proud museums.

It could be argued that distinctive towns and cities are a thing of the past, and indeed many Southern urban places have only photographs to remind them of better days. But the effects of the historic preservation movement, continuing efforts to revitalize town centers, neighborhood conservation work, and, more recently, a return to an architecture more expressive of particular place have all helped reverse the tendency to anonymity. Think of lower Canal Street and the riverfront in New Orleans, once desolate and now an intriguing promenade along the Mississippi. Consider San Antonio, over decades struggling to secure its historic fabric and to give life to a quiet little river, now one of the great destinations in the South and the nation.

Even in dynamic Atlanta, where the past has only lately begun to be given its due, Peachtree Street sprouts skyscrapers while just to either side the tree-shaded neighborhoods of Midtown and Buckhead keep their peace within view of the towers. The street follows a ridge, an ancient path, even as it emerges as a startling new urban linear place.

And on the Florida Gulf Coast, the town of Seaside has captured the imagination of the South and the nation. This new town is being built following a simple but effective code based on the character of older towns. Though the site is only eighty acres, the physical impact of Seaside is a powerful argument that plans based upon a larger idea of place can have profound impact. It plants the idea that new towns or city districts might be made with a flavor we identify only with the old.

Many of the South's cities and towns are true places, or have places within them worthy of the name. Some are historic, some emerging. If the region's longer history was rooted in the land, its future falls clearly in towns and in the metropolitan realm. Today, the South counts 124 metropolitan areas. Thirteen are one million or more in population. But it is the variety of urban areas of medium to smaller size that characterize the region. Will they reflect their historic roots, their geography, their local culture? Will they be true places, or merely statistical areas? The cities and towns in this chapter suggest that saving or making memorable urban places is a challenge worth accepting.

—Philip Morris

*C*harleston, South Carolina, founded in 1670, was the Southern bastion of the British American empire. As a thriving port and export center for rice, indigo, and, later, cotton, the city was the dominant urban settlement in the South from 1730 to 1820. Prosperous merchants built fine houses and places of business in the English styles of the period. But the city, with Caribbean influences, developed a particular galleried house type and wove gardens into the fabric of the town. This view along Broad Street shows the celebrated Four Corners of Law with the steeple of St. Michael's punctuating the scene.

*M*obile, Alabama's, Old Dauphin Way historic neighborhood embodies the garden district character that predominated even the core of most Southern towns and cities. House styles vary, but large porches and deep roof overhangs give continuity to the district.

*G*eorge Washington surveyed and laid out the townsite for Alexandria, Virginia, in 1749. He later attended church there on a regular basis. This historic city, just across the Potomac River from Washington, D.C., was to have been included in the new Capitol district, but was returned to Virginia in 1847. Once a bustling port for tobacco, the town is now favored as a residential suburb of the capital. With more than 450 protected historic structures setting the character, new structures have been required by law to respond to the essentially eighteenth-century texture and scale of the town. Most foreground structures have been built since 1960.

*J*ohnson Square, with its formal plan, canopy of live oaks, and banks of azaleas, is one of more than twenty squares that create focal points for Savannah districts. This square is in the heart of downtown.

*J*ames Oglethorpe gave Savannah, Georgia, a distinctive plan of multiple squares connected by a grid of streets when established in 1733. The squares, and a dramatic waterfront defined by major warehouses, have been revitalized with tourism, now an important local industry. Shipping remains a significant part of the city's economy.

Located on a plateau between the Blue Ridge and the Great Smoky mountains, Asheville, North Carolina, was an early trading center but began to develop as a health resort in the mid-nineteenth century. It was a boom city in the 1920s, fired by speculation, and from the Great Depression on most of its buildings were kept with little alteration. Recent efforts at restoration and revitalization are building on this concentration of early-twentieth-century architecture.

*W*oodrow Wilson's birthplace is Staunton, Virginia, a city in the western region of that state, which served as a trading center for Appalachian region expansion. The city has intensively worked to restore its entire historic center, which includes Mary Baldwin College, housed in the ivory-painted buildings on the hill in this view.

*A*tlanta's Peachtree Street spine, which follows a ridge for much of its length, stands in dramatic contrast to the tree-canopied neighborhoods that surround it. While Atlanta has, for most of its history, been an aggressively modern place and many of these structures have been built only in the past few decades, the force of geography and the local cultural focus on Peachtree as an almost mythic phenomenon have contributed to its urban form. Indeed, the street follows what was originally an Indian trail. Founded in 1847, Atlanta boomed first as a railroad center and more recently as an airline and highway hub. (overleaf)

*F*ounded in 1718, New Orleans remained within the boundaries of its original town plan centered on what is now called Jackson Square. But after being sold to the United States as part of the Louisiana Purchase in 1803, the city boomed from a population of eight thousand to more than 100,000 in 1850. Native French-background residents tended to isolate themselves in the old town, while brash newcomers established what was called the American sector across Canal Street. The tension between the two is a pleasurable one today with intimate buildings and streets of the protected Vieux Carré in contrast to central business district skyscrapers.

*T*he most planned city in the South and in the United States is Washington, D.C., a combination of European baroque and American grid laid out by French-born Major Pierre Charles L'Enfant in 1791. Pennsylvania Avenue, one of the great diagonal boulevards which connects important public buildings or spaces, leads from the Capitol to the White House. Though compromised in part, the plan's spirit was recovered during the McMillan Commission's city beautification movement at the turn of the century when, among other moves, a roughly twelve-story height limit was imposed across the city to assure public monuments and buildings would predominate. More recently, the Pennsylvania Avenue Development Corporation has overseen a sophisticated revitalization of the street, balancing existing landmarks with new buildings in a magnificently upgraded public setting.

*R*eviving districts, such as Birmingham's Five Points South, has brought new life to a growing number of Southern cities. A once-declining neighborhood commercial area, Five Points South has seen major public spaces improved, historic buildings inventoried and renovated, and new buildings and uses introduced. The pedestrian scale and period character of once-neglected districts contribute to their popularity. While cars pass through Five Points South, the primary forms of recreation are walking, sitting, and watching people.

*T*he broad St. Johns River creates a powerful organizing element in Jacksonville, Florida, where a series of stunning bridges connects city districts. Major new developments and public waterfront improvements have recently revitalized the river edge. Earlier towns had been located on the site, but in 1822, a new city was planned in honor of Andrew Jackson, then territorial governor.

*T*he title Oldest European City in the United States belongs to St. Augustine, Florida, established in 1565. Ceded with Florida to the United States by Spain in 1821, St. Augustine in the late nineteenth century took on its present character with the establishment of major resort hotels by Henry Flagler. Though put to varied uses, many of these Spanish Colonial Revival buildings remain to flavor the city.

*T*he most important Spanish and Mexican settlement in Texas, San Antonio grew from a mission outpost to an important trade center, especially after the arrival of the railroad in 1877. In addition to Hispanic and Anglo cultures, the city attracted a large German population. Over the past several decades, protection of historic buildings, such as the Alamo and La Villita, and sensitive development of the San Antonio River have made the city an appealing destination.

*F*ounded first as Fort Nashborough in 1779, Nashville developed as an important western city and became the capital of Tennessee in 1843. As home of Vanderbilt University and other educational institutions, Nashville billed itself as the "Athens of the South" and celebrated its centennial as a city in 1897 with an exposition centered on a reproduction of the Parthenon. Intended to be temporary, the structure has recently been restored and fitted with a full-scale reproduction of Phidias's statue Athena Parthenos.

*S*mall towns are an ingrained aspect of the South, and even with demographic changes and economic challenges, many residents find their discreet charms still appealing. Camden, South Carolina (population approximately 7,500), was settled in the 1730s by English colonists. The town was burned by Sherman's troops, but it retains today the essentially civilized qualities embodied in this image with its gentle progression from sidewalk to fenced yard to front porch to house.

*B*ased on the scale, organization, and civic space of the nineteenth- and early-twentieth-century Southern small town, the town of Seaside, Florida, has captured the imagination of many during its recent development. Designed by architects Andres Duany and Elizabeth Flater-Zyberk for developer Robert Davis, Seaside has begun to serve as the model for others who wish to see new places created worthy of the word "town," not just another subdivision. The power of the model is that it has been built quickly, according to its original vision, and that its parts do add up to something much greater. It is a new place of a character many thought could no longer be achieved.

In The Public Realm

Public buildings are both functional and symbolic centers of the very meaning of community.

In 1887, when Texas created its largest county, Brewster, in the Rio Grande's Big Bend area, a county seat barely existed. The designated town was described about that time as "three buildings surrounded by solitude and spitted on a shimmering spear of steel that was a railroad."

Only a year later, however, Brewster County built a two-story brick courthouse. It still stands.

Public buildings are important in giving meaning and presence to a place. A community on any scale, whether a state, county, or town, is simply not complete and is definitely not as permanent until it has a capitol, courthouse, or city hall. Without public buildings, there is little more than a gaggle of houses and shops. Public buildings are anchors, places that are both functional and symbolic centers of the very meaning of community.

Most people share a common image of public buildings. Courthouses may be the most distinct. According to tradition, they sit in tree-shaded public squares that interrupt the street pattern in the center of town. Columns signal a ceremonial entrance, and a dome encircles the world of legal matters inside. Flags fly. Monuments populate the grounds.

(The Confederate memorial typically is topped with a soldier in battle dress facing north.) In truth, however, it is irrelevant whether or not a courthouse has columns and a dome. The fact that so many people share a common image is an indication of the place a courthouse has in a community. For a courthouse may have a mansard roof. It may be Georgian, Art Deco, or just about any other style, as long as it has not been shuffled off to the suburbs or turned on its end in a new high-rise office tower. Citizens usually are disturbed when seats of government look like community colleges or corporate headquarters. That is because image is one of a public building's main roles. The symbolism of public buildings is a concern that transcends styles and time.

In designing the Virginia capitol in Richmond, the first full-size building in the world to duplicate the Greek temple form, Thomas Jefferson recalled his ancient European model, the Maison Carrée: "It is very simple, yet it . . . would have done honor to our country, as presenting to travellers a specimen of our taste in our infancy, and promising much for our maturer age." Jefferson said his goal in choosing the Greek temple was "to improve the taste of my countrymen, to increase their reputation, to reconcile to them the respect of the world, and procure them its praise."

Nearly 150 years later, the architects of the Louisiana capitol tower in Baton Rouge reflected on the building's symbolism. The capitol, they said, springs from a "broad, substantial base, expressing the material resources of Louisiana and the historic struggles and achievements of her people, buttressing and sustaining the tower rising majestically toward the Heavens, symbolizing the lofty aims and ambitions of sovereign people, guided and influenced by self-restraint and self-improvement, to realization of higher and loftier spiritual goals."

Early settlers recognized the important role public buildings played in the lands they colonized. They claimed land in the name of God and King, and colonization was a means of extending a European nation's influence and power into the New World. Spanish settlers in the Southwest, in fact, were required by law to follow set patterns for town development, which placed government buildings near a central square. Under Mexican government, the laws were still more specific. The block to the west of the square was to contain municipal buildings; the block to the east was to contain religious buildings. In the Southeast, Virginia mandated town plans for county seats, but most states had no such laws for town development. Custom, however, dictated common arrangements for courthouses. They usually were located on large lots on one side of the main street in an open square created by

clipping the corners of the central street intersection, or in a central square which was circled by other streets. Courthouses also could be located at T-shaped intersections, on hilltops, or in other prominent locations. Capitols usually followed similar patterns, especially the central square, though they often were the result of more grand and thorough city planning. Such schemes often designated sites as well for the governor's residence, penitentiaries (jail sites often were specified in county seat plans), asylums, arsenals, and other government buildings.

Thanks to the prominence given to a public building, its location played a major role in organizing a community. A capitol or a courthouse in a square was key to the street plan. The building helped a community attain a stronger foothold in the wilderness. And it helped establish a town's importance over other communities. As a result, promoters of new communities sometimes donated land for courthouses or other public buildings to ensure the stability and viability of their towns. A courthouse brought citizens to town on county business, increasing the trade for local merchants. Within the town, a courthouse—especially one on a square—affected land values nearby, as those businesses facing the square would have a higher visibility and receive more trade than would businesses on another street.

County seats generally remain the most prominent communities in many counties, though occasionally other towns grow larger as a result of the presence of universities, transportation,

industry, or other developments unrelated to government. The state capital, on the other hand, often is not the largest city in the state. This is partially due to changing patterns of economic development and the fact that capital cities often were chosen—or created—principally for their central locations.

Among the original colonies, capitals often were relocated expressly to remove the government from its earlier English-designated site. As states grew westward from their initial coastal settlements, capitals often were moved several times. Virginia, North Carolina, South Carolina, and Georgia all moved their capitals west.

Like county seats, state capitals enjoyed a prominence that sometimes created a rivalry for the seat of government. A grand city and county building plan unveiled for Louisville in 1835, for example, was intended to establish a government complex that would lure the state capital from Frankfort, though the effort failed. Alabama abandoned one capital site because frequent river flooding made it uninhabitable. By the mid-nineteenth century, most Southern state capitals had been established. Oklahoma was the last to move, relocating from Guthrie to Oklahoma City in 1910.

Today, most of the region's capitol buildings—with the conspicuous exception of Louisiana's tower—are domed and columned Greek or Classical Revival structures. That was not always the case. Virginia's early capitol at Williamsburg, which has been rebuilt as part of the town restoration, is a Georgian building with two stories and a usable attic with dormers, small by the standards of today's capitols but substantial at the time. North Carolina's seat of English government, Tryon Palace in New Bern, also reconstructed, is a larger, grander Georgian structure befitting the Crown's representative in the colony.

Some states had less auspicious beginnings. After selecting Austin as its capital city, Texas first built a frame capitol that looked like a huge dogtrot-style cabin. Then came a modest Greek Revival building that was derided as a "corn crib with a pumpkin on top." Finally, the state erected its present capitol, a classical structure so large it housed the entire state government well into the twentieth century and so grand that its dome rises higher than the dome of the U.S. Capitol in Washington, D.C.

A Georgian building with a tall, dome-like cupola, Maryland's State House in Annapolis, built between 1772 and 1779, is the oldest state house in the nation still in use. Virginia's capitol in Richmond, built between 1785 and 1792, was an important break from the English styles of building, for it established the Greek Revival style as the dominant form of public building in the United States. Greek Revival was seen as an appropriate style for the young country, as Greece had created the democratic type of government. Capitols built in such forms were viewed as "temples of democracy." Courthouses in the style were seen as "temples of justice."

The progression of capitol styles, however, is best seen in those states that have left their earlier buildings standing with the new. In Frankfort, Kentucky, the Old State House, completed in 1830, is the third statehouse. The first two burned. The small Greek Revival capitol, with a cupola that still is the building's main source of light, served until the early twentieth century, when a new capitol was built. It consisted of Georgia, Tennessee, and Italian marble, a four-hundred-foot-long interior vista, and a staircase modeled after those in the Grand Opera House in Paris. In Little Rock, Arkansas, the Greek Revival Old State House, begun in 1833, overlooks the Arkansas River on a small urban site; the new Classical Revival capitol, begun in 1900 and requiring sixteen years, seven governors, and four Capitol Commissions to finish, rises imposingly from a hill west of downtown. In Baton Rouge, Louisiana, the new tower capitol coexists with the old capitol, a Gothic fortress built between 1847 and 1849. Georgia also has a Gothic old capitol (Georgia's and Louisiana's were the only two Gothic capitols in the country), completed in 1807 in Milledgeville. The legislature met there until 1868, when it moved to the gold-domed capitol in Atlanta. North Carolina and Florida both have striking new halls for their governing bodies. In Raleigh, the state of North Carolina built its Legislative Building in 1963, rather than add to its 1840 Greek Revival capitol. The old building was restored and still houses the governor's office. In Tallahassee, the state of Florida built a capitol tower in 1977 behind the old capitol, which was constructed in 1845 and recently restored.

Courthouses and other buildings for local government show an even greater range of styles than capitols. Some are different because of the cultures that produced them. The Cabildo, the hall for the Town Council built in Jackson Square in New Orleans between 1795 and 1799, is a structure of decidedly French origins, with a mansard roof and an arcade on the ground floor. Others take their styles from the period in which they were built. Many counties first had log courthouses. Few of these still exist, and those that do are museums, such as the Comanche County Courthouse in Comanche, Texas.

Many counties have had a succession of courthouses, built as earlier structures burned, became dilapidated, or grew out of fashion. Courthouse construction seems to have come in waves, prompted by local prosperity, expansion into western territories, or government programs, such as the Works Progress Administration during the Depression. Arkansas, for example, built only three courthouses during the 1980s but fourteen in the 1900s, twenty-two in the 1930s but only one in the 1950s. The most common style in that state was Georgian Revival, followed by Classical Revival, Modern, and Art Deco. But courthouses also were built in eight other styles, including Greek Revival, Italian Villa, Chateauesque, and Richardsonian Romanesque.

Courthouses play an integral part in local life. The Rhea County Courthouse in Dayton, Tennessee, was the scene of the Scopes "monkey" trial. In Vicksburg, Mississippi, and Petersburg,

Virginia, courthouses played roles in Civil War sieges of those cities. Union troops were held captive in the courthouse in Vicksburg; troops from both armies are said to have told time by the clock tower in the Petersburg courthouse.

Aside from their style, their historical significance, and their day-to-day business function, all courthouses are symbolically important to their home counties. Courthouses symbolize their functions—law and justice—and they symbolize the county's history, pride, and affluence. These messages are conveyed through the building's site, scale, quality, style, architectural elements (such as domes), ornamentation (such as sculptures of Blind Justice), and monuments.

In the 1950s and 1960s, modernist architectural styles eliminated such symbolism. Along with other types of buildings, courthouses were seen as functional tools. Parking, office space, and cost took precedence over symbolism and the building's intangible role in the community. Some were demolished and new government centers were built instead on the edge of town. Others were replaced in town by towers or were severely remodeled. In recent years, however, the historic preservation movement has helped counties across the South recognize the value of their old courthouses and their importance in creating an identity and a sense of place.

In a rural county, the courthouse is often the most elaborate building in the county. It is the center of activity. If there is a town square, citizens sit on its tree-shaded benches or pause to read inscriptions on monuments there. The buildings around the square likely have been restored. Their storefronts are still prime retail locations; their second-story offices still are popular with attorneys.

Even in a city, where commercial and institutional buildings have long since overshadowed the courthouse, an old courthouse is a reminder of past days, a symbolic community anchor. In times when citizens do much of their county business by mail or on the telephone and the number of people who use the buildings on a daily basis is proportionately small, the courthouse retains its importance. Jury duty remains a right, a privilege, and a duty. Record keeping is essential to an organized society. The principles of law, justice, and democratic government remain strong. And public buildings live as symbolic centers of community life in the South.

—Ernest Wood

50 PUBLIC BUILDINGS

*M*onuments—especially Civil War monuments—are an important part of Southern capitol grounds and courthouse squares. The South Carolina capitol, however, is itself a reminder of the war. The building was under construction when the war began, but work did not stop until fighting actually reached Columbia in 1865. Shots from the guns of Union General William Sherman's troops hit the new walls but caused little damage. Today, six bronze stars mark the scars from the cannonade.

*P*ublic buildings also stand as monuments to historical events. In Vicksburg, Mississippi, the courthouse contains a museum recalling the Civil War siege of the river city.

*T*he Texas capitol is like the state—expansive, exuberant, reveling in its local materials, and proud of the innovative deal that got it built. The first capitol in Austin was a single-story pine structure surrounded by a stockade and a ditch to protect it from Mexican and Indian attacks. Today's capitol, completed in 1888, is the state's third seat of government. It is nearly six times as large as its predecessor and taller than the Capitol in Washington. It housed nearly the entire state government until the 1920s. The capitol complex now spreads over dozens of buildings in downtown Austin.

The North Carolina capitol remains virtually unchanged since it was built in 1840. The capitol's importance to earlier citizens is indicated by its original cost—more than three times the state's yearly income. More recently, the state's regard for the structure is indicated by its decision to build a new Legislative building, rather than expand the capitol, and to restore the old building.

The Nelson County Courthouse in Bardstown, Kentucky, sits at the intersection of the town's four major streets. The arrangement is a common one in the South. The courthouse becomes not only an important symbol of government and community but a key element in shaping the town plan.

Even a simple public building such as the Moore County Courthouse in Lynchburg, Tennessee, is an important town centerpiece. Architectural details, such as a cupola, and the building's location give the courthouse an importance that no other structure can have.

*E*xcept for the cars, the courthouse square in Granbury, Texas, looks nearly as it did one hundred years ago. The 1891 Hood County Courthouse and most of the buildings around it have been restored, and the entire square is listed on the National Register of Historic Places.

*A*rchitectural detailing reflects the period in which a building was erected. Turn-of-the-century wealth from cotton farming helped finance sculpture and other ornate details on the McLennan County Courthouse in Waco, Texas.

*P*atterned after the U.S. Capitol, the Arkansas capitol has a familiar look. States often struggled to build such imposing edifices, however. Begun in 1900, the Arkansas building took sixteen years to complete. The original capitol, built in 1833 on the banks of the Arkansas River in downtown Little Rock, is now a museum.

A Cultivated Culture

As surely as Scarlett pulled up a radish to quell her hunger, we look to the garden to nourish our body and our spirit as well. For food or fancy, Southerners are apt to turn a shovelful of soil.

In the South, summer days are long, and so is the season. No wonder we have always planted gardens. In an agricultural community, growing plants is a way of life. In more urban areas, a garden provides a link to nature that might otherwise be lost. The garden can take you from childhood to retirement. It is a place to climb trees and make forts, a setting for weddings and reunions, and a spot for those roses you have never had the time to grow.

The role of a garden varies with history and with gardeners. Among the gentry of the eighteenth century, a garden was apt to be a maze of boxwoods or a drive lined with live oaks. It was order in the wilderness. In fact, the earliest homes had bare, swept-earth yards with no plants next to the house. Although it may seem surprising today (FHA requires a foundation planting for new homes), it was perfectly logical. In an untamed land, shrubs were hiding places for trouble that came on both two and four legs.

Southerners love picket fences and the fragrant roses that scamper over them. But in days gone by, those pickets were designed to keep out as much as they kept in. Since herbs and vegetables were essential to medicines and meals, the gardener had to protect his crop from grazing livestock.

To the pioneer, the Confederate, the Depression farmer, and the victory gardeners of World War II, the garden was survival—vegetables enough to eat fresh and more for "puttin' up." Not only were these gardens essential to the nutrition of the region, but they influenced the regional cuisine. The long hot summers of the Deep South are ideal for okra, watermelon, crowder peas, and sweet potatoes. Corn is ground into grits and meal. And peaches and pecans leave their mark on the Southern landscape, as well as on the menu.

For the first Southerners who arrived by ship, seeds were precious cargo. They were insurance against hunger in this new land and a tie to a culture left behind. Each year these seeds were planted and the vegetables harvested, but the earliest, biggest, and most vigorous plants were reserved to produce the seeds for next year's crop. Many of these vegetables have become family heirlooms and are still grown today.

Those who gardened in isolation on the frontier of settlement depended on friends, family, and a few early seed companies to send a "start" of seeds through the mail. As communities grew, gardeners began to buy seeds metered out of bins at farm supply stores. Now gardeners can pick up a packet at the garden center. Of course, they swap seeds and cuttings with neighbors. But the more zealous prefer to order through the mail, just like their forebears.

Today the garden is most often a landscape in the smallest sense of the word. It becomes a setting for the house and defines the boundary of the lot. What comes between—a pool, vegetable patch, flower bed, azaleas, terrace, barbeque pit, or a tidy green lawn—is the expression of the owner and a reflection of a life-style.

It is probably no coincidence that the advent of "low maintenance" gardens coincided with the baby boom. The veterans returned, families grew, and they had precious little time for anything more than mowing the grass. Convenience foods became the order of the day, so why not convenience gardens, too?

Now the babies are grown, with homes of their own. Many are rediscovering the pleasure of gardening. However, their purpose is different. Instead of gardening to feed the family, they garden to have the freshest lettuce, the best tomatoes, and the exercise that comes with them.

The Southern landscape is as diverse and beautiful as any other area of the country. And whether you address the landscape of nature or the landscape of man, you find that the South has a look all its own.

Broadleaf evergreens abound in nature, and gardeners will find even more at the nursery. Until a Southerner travels north or west, the evergreen stage where we live our lives is scarcely noticed, let alone appreciated. While other regions have needle-leaf evergreens, ours is a different texture, big-leaved and lush.

Many of the South's favorite plants were not native, but introduced since the 1800s. Crape myrtles, gardenias, and camellias are foreign, but they have become essential to the Southern identity. And evergreen azaleas, with their Oriental origins, are the very signature of a Southern spring.

Southerners cherish history, particularly personal history. The gardens of the South hold many relics of times past. You may find a bench from Mother's garden, a camellia from Grandmother's garden, or even an architectural remnant of a landmark now gone.

As a landscape designer in North Carolina explains, for many Southerners, gardening is a way to keep memories alive. We let go of things very, very slowly. And a garden is one way of accepting those changes while keeping pieces of our family history alive.

In fact, we hold on to our past tenaciously. Hence, the numerous restorations of historic gardens. Whether they are grand limestone designs or small farmhouse gardens, they hold a story of a family and of our region. Bok Tower, Brookgreen Gardens, Dumbarton Oaks, Biltmore House and Gardens, Tryon Palace, Monticello. These are our heritage where wealth and grand design teamed to leave us inspiration. But visit the Mordecai House in Raleigh, the Tullie Smith House in Atlanta, the Brush-Everard House in Colonial Williamsburg, or Tuckahoe Plantation outside Richmond, you will find design that is beautiful in its simplicity and ageless appeal.

In some ways, new gardens are much the same as the old in that their owners seek the same feeling of permanence. Moss is welcomed in the corner of a walk, and it is good when white concrete ages to a comfortable gray. Thanks to our warmth and moisture, a garden can achieve a sense of age within a few years.

However, a few years cannot substitute for the generations that have passed since the live oaks of Oak Alley or Afton Villa were planted. We are the recipients of a legacy, and we have a responsibility to future generations.

Gardening helps us understand our bequest—the land, the environment, and ourselves. Gardeners learn, if only by trial and error, that we are participants in the processes of nature.

Hours in the garden are peaceful. Turn the soil, snip the faded blooms, or discover a forgotten favorite pushing through the soil. The activity is healthful for body and spirit. It gives pause for solitude, occupies the hands while the mind works over the affairs of life, and sets free creativity that may not otherwise find expression. This is why we garden and why generations before us have cultivated the Southern soil.

—Linda Askey Weathers

Spring greens and foxglove flourish in the black earth of Old Salem, a restored Moravian community in Winston-Salem, North Carolina.

For all of Thomas Jefferson's worldliness, he was fascinated by the humble task of gardening. Old-fashioned flowers abound in the flower borders that surround the lawn at Monticello. The little pond near the South Pavilion was a holding area for fish destined for the dinner table.

*G*arden gates are the purest sort of intrigue. In Charleston, South Carolina, a gate left ajar means visitors are welcome; ironically, only a few will enter. This freestanding gate adds a charming focal point to a lush garden setting.

*T*he trumpet vine is as much a part of summer in the South as bare feet and barbeque. A gift of nature, it scampered over trees and brush long before man built fences for it to adorn.

*S*haded corridors lead to secluded courtyards between Charleston's historic homes. The space between houses, originally designed for cooling and to prevent the spread of fires, offers a refreshing oasis for relaxing and for gardening.

In 1890, George Washington Vanderbilt began a country house in the North Carolina mountains. Five years and 250 rooms later, he had a Christmas party to formally mark its opening. Now, visitors to Biltmore House marvel at both its enormous scale and its exquisite detail. Landscape architect Frederick Law Olmsted, who designed Central Park, laid out Biltmore's gardens, parklike environs, and three-mile approach road.

The Pebble Garden at Dumbarton Oaks in Washington, D. C., is an intricate mosaic made from thousands of rounded stones. A thin sheet of water heightens the stones' natural colors.

Water trickles between rock obstacles below. Branches hang overhead, still in the morning air. This is the Japanese Garden at the Fort Worth Botanic Gardens. Visitors pause to watch the brilliant koi that school below the bridge and to enjoy the foliage as it colors autumn days.

The Reflecting Pool Garden at Winterthur Museum and Gardens in Winterthur, Delaware, mirrors autumn colors in its tranquil water setting.

Paul Manship's bronze Goliath Heron *and* Crowned Crane *stand guard at the entrance to the Small Sculpture Gallery at Brookgreen Gardens near Murrells Inlet, South Carolina.*

The fresh scent of boxwood is the garden's cologne at the Brush-Everard House in Colonial Williamsburg. One touch prompts waves of movement in the boxwoods' supple boughs.

Antenor's Lady *stands gracefully on a stone terrace at Jasmine Hill near Montgomery, Alabama. The original statue stood on the Acropolis until 480 B. C., when the Persians overran Athens.*

The bucket brigade, sent out to put their boundless energy to good use, hunts the fallen pecans. Young backs and sharp eyes are only hampered by short attention spans. But the promise of steaming pies will hold them to the task, as it will the adults who crack and shell one of the South's tastiest crops.

At Cedar Lane Farms near Madison, Georgia, the gardens are in keeping with the nineteenth-century farmhouse. A formal boxwood garden is surrounded by a picket fence, which once served to keep the farm animals at bay. In its day, this pocket of domesticated plants in an untamed land was kept tidy with swept clay walks and clipped boxwood hedges. Flowers and herbs were cultivated in the beds.

*H*uge Southern Indian hybrid azaleas form an understory for live oaks at Afton Villa near St. Francisville, Louisiana.

*W*isteria cloaks this Richmond porch like lace curtains on parlor windows.

Centers For The Arts

***Trod upon the stage or hung upon the wall,
the history of the South is portrayed and protected in its
theaters and museums.***

Culture came early to the South. On February 12, 1736, *The Recruiting Officer* was presented at the Theatre in Dock Street, in Charleston. But this was not the first theater in the colonies. Some twenty years earlier, William Levingston had built a 30-by-86-foot playhouse facing the palace green in Williamsburg. The first play was performed there in 1718 to celebrate King George's birthday.

Indeed, the southern colonies, lacking the puritanical bent of the northern colonies, became the major center for theater in Colonial America. Like much of Colonial life, theater was an English derivative. Touring companies, often trained on the London stage, brought their art to the colonies. Lewis Hallam and his family of players made their debut with Shakespeare's *The Merchant of Venice* in Williamsburg on September 15, 1752. After Hallam's death four years later, David Douglass took over the company and married the widow Hallam. The new group, called The American Company of Comedians, continued touring the southern colonies.

Despite the southern colonies' more open attitude towards actors and the theater, there were restrictions. In fact, Maryland and Virginia were the only colonies not to pass some form of anti-theater legislation. Then on October 22, 1774, the Continental Congress, meeting in Philadelphia, banned horse racing, cockfighting, gaming, and plays. Theater went into hiatus until after the Revolution.

By 1790, touring companies were back in business, making the circuit. John Bignall and Thomas Wade West brought a group of actors over from London to form the Virginia Company of Comedians, which played to audiences in Richmond, Norfolk, Petersburg, and Alexandria. Local theater buildings were often financed by local subscription and used as a combination public meeting hall and theater. When the professional troops were not in town, amateur groups used the facilities for their performances.

Then on the day after Christmas, 1811, a tragic fire at the Richmond Theatre claimed the lives of over seventy people, including Virginia Governor George William Smith. A public outcry against theaters darkened stages across the South once again.

After the end of the War of 1812, footlights came on again, both along the Atlantic Seaboard and in the newly opened southern interior. One troop, led by Samuel Drake, entertained audiences in the Kentucky frontier. Another company, based in New Orleans, called on cities along the Mississippi as far north as St. Louis. Gradually, these traveling repertory companies expanded their circuits to include most of the larger towns of the interior South. Other troops took advantage of the newly invented steamboat to ply their craft. Showboats, theaters on barges, could be towed or pushed by steamboats up and down the rivers of the South, where they brought entertainment to smaller communities well into the twentieth century.

But it was the development of the railroad in the days after the Civil War that allowed the great stars of the day to travel across the country on whistle-stop tours. Soon, nearly every town and city had its opera house. Surviving examples include the Springer Opera House in Columbus, Georgia, the Grand Opera House in Wilmington, Delaware, the Garden Theatre in Charleston, South Carolina, and the Bijou in Knoxville. Typical was Macon's 1884 Academy of Music, which was remodeled in 1905 and renamed the Grand Opera House. From its 2,418 seats, patrons enjoyed diverse celebrities such as Sarah Bernhardt, Lillian Gish, Will Rogers, Burns and Allen, and Houdini.

The second, and greatest, period of theater growth occurred in the early decades of the twentieth century. The new phenomenon of moving pictures was sweeping the country, and over four thousand new theaters were built to accommodate the rapidly growing American movie audiences. Competing for the crowds, each new theater tried to outdo the competition by being grander, more elaborate, and more elegant than its rivals. Architectural inspiration for the movie palaces came from a wide, and sometimes unlikely, range of idioms. The baroque palaces of Europe were the inspiration for some movie houses such as the Orpheum in Memphis (1928). The ruins of an earlier Mexican civilization were the inspiration for the Aztec in San Antonio (1926). The Fox in Atlanta (1929) is loosely based on Middle Eastern architecture and features an onion dome outside and minarets inside. A popular and spectacular feature of many of the movie palaces was the "sky" ceiling over the auditorium. The blue-painted ceiling usually included twinkling "star" lights and even moving clouds projected on the ceiling. These atmospheric theaters were the development of St. Louis architect John Eberson, who designed the Majestic in San Antonio, the Tampa and the Olympia in Miami. His Majestic Theatre in Houston was the country's first atmospheric theater.

But the Great Depression and World War II brought an end to the great movie palaces. Many closed their doors as their audiences moved to the suburbs. Others struggled on as revival houses. The wrecker's ball claimed others. But in the last twenty years, the preservation movement has embraced both movie palaces and opera houses. Coupled with the new theaters and performing arts centers, the footlights are once again shining brightly across the South.

America's first museum, the Charleston Museum, began in 1773 as an offshoot of the Library Society, which had been founded in the South Carolina city in 1743. The Charleston Museum was a natural history museum, after the model of the British Museum.

One of the earliest art museums, and the oldest museum building in the country, is Baltimore's Peale Museum, built in 1814. The founder of the museum was, appropriately enough, named Rembrandt Peale, who was a member of a family of artists and museum promoters. His father, Charles Willson Peale (1741-1827), had opened his own museum, the first in the new republic, in Philadelphia in 1786 to display his paintings of Revolutionary War figures. Rembrandt's brothers opened museums in New York City and Utica.

In 1829, a British mineralogist died, leaving in his will his entire fortune to the United States, a country he had never visited. He had been born James Macie, illegitimate son of Hugh Smithson Percy, First Duke of Northumberland, and Elizabeth Keate Macie. At Oxford, he proved to be quite a genius at science and, at twenty-two, was the youngest person ever admitted to membership in the Royal Society. Inheriting a considerable fortune from his mother, he worked as a scientist and, late in life, changed his name to James Smithson. His remarkable gift to America " . . . to found at Washington, under the name of the Smithsonian Institution, an establishment for the increase and diffusion of knowledge . . . " totaled over £100,000.

In 1846, Congress established the institution that bears his name. It was to go on to become America's attic, the keeper of all things great and small.

"Museums by bequest" was to be the pattern for the establishment of American (and Southern) museums over the next century, as the captains of industry played out the role of European royalty. But where the crowned heads of Europe collected for themselves, the art of the American aristocracy was, at least after their deaths, to be enjoyed by all the people.

Georgetown banker William Wilson Corcoran (1798-1888) was an avid collector of art, especially the work of American painters. His fortune made, he retired in 1854 and started work on his museum. Delayed by the Civil War (and Corcoran's Southern sympathies), the gallery did not open until 1874 in a building designed by architect James Renwick. The museum in Washington now bears his, not Corcoran's, name.

Other benefactors of the arts include Charles Freer, railroad and car manufacturer, who donated his collection of Oriental art and paintings by James Whistler. The Freer Gallery of Art in Washington, D.C., is now part of the Smithsonian Institution.

The Kress brothers, Samuel, Claude, and Ross, of dime-store fame were givers on a grand scale to a number of Southern museums. Their extensive collections, especially of early Italian Renaissance paintings, became important components not only of the National Gallery of Art in Washington, D.C., but also of city museums in Memphis,
Birmingham, Atlanta, Columbia, Raleigh, Houston, Miami, and Tulsa.

But Southern museums were not always the result of civic largess. In 1947, the North Carolina legislature appropriated a million dollars for the purchase of paintings, the first state to do so. Bolstered by art from the Kress collection, the North Carolina Museum of Art opened its doors in 1956 in a recycled government office building in Raleigh. In many other Southern cities, museums combined the efforts of local government and private groups to provide the funds for building, art acquisition, and ongoing programs.

But museums can take many forms. A house, rooted in the history of a city, can become both a symbol of the community and a way to explain the day-to-day life of another era. The grand houses of the rich and famous or the simple, modest homes of more ordinary folk, each has its story to tell. Other museums focus on the life and deeds of a single person or on a particular aspect of Southern culture and history. Still other museums look to the future as well as the past, as they explain the science and technology that have changed, and continue to change, the face of the South.

—Louis Joyner

Charleston's first theater, the Theatre in Dock Street, opened February 12, 1736, with the play The Recruiting Officer. *Colonial and antebellum theaters were often financed by local subscription and used for both amateur performances and touring professional companies. The present structure, a 1930s WPA project, is a conjectural reconstruction of the original.*

In the age of the railroads, every Southern city had its elegant opera house where the luminaries of the day came to entertain. Such greats as Edwin Booth, John Philip Sousa, Martha Graham, Irving Berlin, and Agnes De Mille graced the stage of Columbus, Georgia's, Springer Opera House.

The invention of motion pictures brought an era of fantasy to theaters across the nation. Architectural inspirations included baroque European palaces, Moorish and Spanish styles, Middle Eastern, and even Aztec. Some movie palaces, such as Loew's Theater in Richmond, featured a plaster "sky" complete with twinkling "stars" and projected "clouds."

The Smithsonian's first building, completed in 1855, was designed by architect James Renwick, Jr., in the Norman style. The "castle" is now part of a complex of museums and galleries that line both sides of the National Mall.

In 1947, North Carolina became the first state to appropriate funds for a public art collection. That million dollars was the start of the North Carolina Museum of Art. First housed in the old state highway building downtown, the museum moved to its new suburban quarters in 1983.

The history of the South is an important component of many museums. At the Museum of the Confederacy in Richmond, a red officer's kepi and a captured model 1861 Savage pistol share the display case with a drum and Confederate battle flag.

Fort Worth's Kimbell Art Museum began with the generosity of a local philanthropist, businessman Kay Kimbell. The museum collects pivotal works from antiquity to the twentieth century, including this rose-granite statue of an Egyptian king.

architecture, denominations and beliefs determined a church's style more than its locale. As settlers moved west, into the Black Belt of Alabama and Mississippi, for example, they built churches like those they recalled from their homes in Virginia, the Carolinas, or Georgia. So churches across the South often are similar—and neighboring churches often are strikingly different.

No matter what their style, however, most nineteenth-century churches were small, single-room buildings with rows of pews facing a central pulpit. Their main role was to provide a place for preaching.

This role, and as a result church architecture, was to change once again in the late nineteenth and the twentieth centuries, with the advent of the Sunday school movement. What began as a movement to teach children to read the Bible grew into a seemingly endless parade of men's and women's groups, choirs, and service guilds. Churches offered classrooms and meeting halls to scout troops and other community organizations. Charitable groups serving the community were based in churches. These changes came first and were most common in the cities. As a result, few of the old-fashioned, one-room churches remain in urban areas. But in the country, the evolution is obvious. Pleasant Hill Baptist Church in central Alabama, for example, built its sanctuary in about 1850. In the 1950s, it added Sunday school wings and connected them to the original structure with breezeways. Across the highway, however, stands a remnant of earlier days. Pleasant Hill

Presbyterian Church, a single-room Greek Revival structure, was built in 1851 and abandoned in 1927. Vacant ever since, it is slowly giving way to the elements and vandalism.

Just as we can read history in the church, so can we read it in the cemetery. Walk through and you will find generations of husbands and wives, sons and daughters, mothers and fathers lovingly memorialized. Revolutionary and Confederate soldiers. Politicians and businessmen. Craftsmen and pioneers. A cross section of Southern society.

Cemeteries are located at churches, on large city blocks, and—in the country—on private property. Years ago, it was not always possible to take the deceased to the church, so plantations and out-of-the-way farms and ranches had their own plots. Those who died in cities could face similar problems, however. Raleigh's original City Cemetery, established in 1798, is divided into quarters—two for city residents; one for blacks, both free and slave; and one for out-of-towners who died while visiting the capital city.

The South's most distinctive cemeteries are those in New Orleans, where a high water table requires aboveground tombs. Some are wall vaults, which stack the tombs together. Other tombs are individual and quite elaborate. Surrounded by wrought iron fences, the marble tombs most commonly resemble miniature Greek temples.

Though cemeteries sometimes are sectioned according to religion and race,

and though each section is further subdivided by family, distinct burial customs prevail. On tombstones, doves and lambs are common Christian symbols, with a lamb indicating the deceased was a child. A weeping willow, which comes from English tradition, is a symbol of mourning. A broken shaft or column indicates the deceased met with an accidental death. Graves usually are oriented east-west, with the foot at the east; this allows the deceased to face Jerusalem when he rises on Judgment Day. (Evildoers sometimes are buried facing the wrong direction as punishment.) Wives customarily are buried on their husband's left, as popular tradition says Eve was made from one of Adam's left ribs.

Old Southern churches and cemeteries are special places because they are spiritual places. For the Southerner today, cemeteries and churches provide a continuity with the past, a link to the lives and beliefs of the Southerners who went before. They are places that open a door to a personal part of the region's history.

—Ernest Wood

The Newbern Presbyterian Church, Hale County, Alabama, follows the Greek Revival style favored by many antebellum Protestant denominations. The simple frame church features separate entrances for men and women.

*B*reaking with other denominations, the Episcopalians believed that Gothic, rather than Greek architecture, was the proper model for a church. The design for St. Andrew's Episcopal Church in Prairie, Alabama, may have come from a pattern book on rural architecture by New York architect Richard Upjohn.

*T*owering over the North Carolina port of Wilmington, the spires of the First Baptist Church and the First Presbyterian Church emphasize the importance of religion in the South. The Presbyterian church was built in 1928 to replace a pre-Civil War church lost to fire. The Baptist church, designed by Samuel Sloan of Philadelphia, was begun in 1859.

*I*n 1720, Franciscan friars founded Mission San José, one of five missions in San Antonio. Much more than a church, the mission was a self-sustaining community that sheltered Spanish colonizers and Indian converts from raiding Apaches and Comanches. The church was constructed of tufa, plastered, and then decorated with bright Moorish designs.

Still in use after two centuries, the Maryland State House dominates the Annapolis skyline. Settled in 1660, the city, named after Princess Anne, was an important Colonial port and, for a short time, served as capital of the Continental Congress.

In the winter of 1811-1812, a series of earthquakes along the New Madrid fault rocked the northwest corner of Tennessee. As the earth's crust fell away, the waters of the nearby Mississippi flooded the area, forming Reelfoot Lake.

*M*ountain Creek Lake at Callaway Gardens provides a quiet refuge in the Georgia Piedmont. Industrialist Cason Callaway established the gardens as a recreational area in the 1950s.

*T*umbling down the rugged mountainside, this stream in the Great Smoky Mountains is a haven for trout and a challenge for the fly fisherman.

*The Sea Islands of the Georgia and South
Carolina coast provided fertile farmland for the
rice, indigo, and cotton crops of Colonial
planters. The salt marshes also provide a rich
feeding and breeding ground for many marine
animals.*

*The sugary sand, deep blue sky, and warm
sun draw visitors of all ages to the South's
beaches. Here on Mexico Beach in the Florida
panhandle, a solitary fisherman patiently
waits for a nibble.*

Good Times
Down Home

Around courthouse squares, at camp meetings, in town and country, Southerners gathered to learn news, conduct business, celebrate with family and friends, and get a little of that old-time religion.

In past centuries Southerners spent long periods alone, many in log cabins on the edge of the frontier, others on plantations far secluded from the hum of town life. But occasionally, they had to gather together, to grind grain, sign papers, marry, bury dead, barter, renew friendships, play games, and learn news. To be apart and yet to seek company was certainly innate of Southerners of Scotch-Irish extraction. Just as they had done already on the Ulster plantation, they felt the need to move to the edge of the frontier to seek room for their stock to roam. Yet, they also felt the clannish tug to seek out their own kind the way they did in their twice-removed homeland of the lowlands of Scotland.

Those gathering places were as informal as the yard of a gristmill down by the river or as structured as the angles of a town square. Yet the function of the space overshadowed the form. Wherever Southerners have gathered, they have created their own social spaces: town square, brush arbor, country store, restaurant, festival grounds, dance hall.

Yet, if those spaces were informal, they nevertheless found a place deep in Southerners' hearts. We preserve some of the earliest gathering places and follow the same time-honored functions of those social settings as if they were ritual.

Camp meetings survive. In Georgia, the Methodist organization still maintains several, including one at Pine Log Methodist Church near Cartersville in the first loping foothills of north Georgia. Just behind the 1830s church, worshipers assemble for a week in August, settling on wooden pews under an open-air pavilion, a structure one step above the brush arbor. Curling around the pavilion is a street of "cabins," actually clapboard and plywood and mostly one-room structures, where families still live for a week.

Country stores survive, too, as much traditional gathering places as retail enterprises. Once, these stores were a singular tie to the outside world for farm families living in the far reaches of the rural South. Shelves were stocked with nearly every item needed—from lard to sewing thread, hames lines to bath oil. Often, the store was the plantation store, where sharecroppers were furnished all their goods, which they repaid after the crop was sold.

As a gathering place, the country store also provided much-needed diversions. Area folks gathered to chat on the porch or around the warmth of the ubiquitous potbellied stove, drummers stopped by with goods, and friends and neighbors gathered for music and dancing. Music still fills the air each Saturday night at Cuzzins General Store on State 127 north of Walhalla in the upcountry of South Carolina. Far up a mountain road, along about sundown, friends and neighbors arrive with banjos, fiddles, and guitars, sit around the gasoline pumps, and bring down the sun with the music of these hills. Tourists from nearby state parks, lakes, and resorts unlimber lawn chairs and nibble picnic suppers, while listening to such tunes as "Kicking Mule," "Shuck the Corn," and "Millie in the Low Ground." A down-home ritual has turned into an up-country tourist attraction.

Saturday night in the South, when work is done, has always been the time to pick up the fiddle and rosin the bow. The work calendar usually determines the times for folks to gather. For a rural, agricultural people to find a few days to gather, those times usually mean mid-to late-summer.

Planters in the South Carolina Low Country traditionally escaped the "sickly season" of summer that seemed to infect their plantations. From frost to frost, they found refuge either on higher

ground or at the seashore. Entire towns were built for seasonal refugees, such as Summerville, just north of Charleston. The mountains were popular, too; the area around Flat Rock, North Carolina, is still called "Little Charleston in the Mountains" because so many residents of the coastal city vacationed there. Pawleys Island, South Carolina, was a popular summer spot for planters. Even today, at least one nineteenth-century beach house remains.

By the mid-twentieth century, vacation towns had arisen along the beaches of the South, populated in summer mainly by high school and college students. Many of these towns follow the same form: beach, boardwalk, motels (now condominiums), and beachtown "strip," a neon bazaar of fast-food outlets, trinket shops, nightclubs, and thrill rides. Especially on summer weekends, such seaside towns as Myrtle Beach, South Carolina, and Panama City, Florida, turn into one large sand-and-asphalt party house. By day, the beaches are thronged; by night, the young vacationers prowl the strip. They gather at such towns to meet new friends, find romance, and get a tan.

Summer, especially July and August, was always the popular gathering time for camp meetings and other festivities. Then, the crops were "laid by," and there was little else to do but leave the fields to the rain and sun. Then friends and neighbors could gather to renew friendships and faith at festivities and camp meetings.

Many festivals in the South take a berth on the midsummer calendar.

Exemplary is the Neshoba County Fair near Philadelphia, Mississippi, a week-long event with a midway, livestock shows, preaching, politicking, singing, and dinner on the grounds. "Mississippi's Giant House Party," as it calls itself, turned one-hundred-years-old in 1989.

The week-long event is part camp meeting and part State fair, and it manages to combine the two diverse types of events in its design. A neon midway forms a street of rides, fried food, and games of chance. Nearby are hay-strewn barns, where youngsters groom pampered livestock for prizes; a hall displaying blue-ribbon preserves and vegetables "put up" by Neshoba County housewives; and a red clay track for Standardbred races.

The heart of the fairgrounds, however, is Founder's Square, which duplicates the camp meeting design. The open-air Founder's Pavilion, with its wooden pews and sawdust floor, is the center of the square, where singing, preaching, and political speechmaking goes on throughout the week. Around the square stand rude cabins, some dating to the fair's earliest days, and many handed down through generations of the same family. These structures have set the architectural style of the fair: tin roof, porches upstairs and downstairs, naked light bulbs, and rooms crowded with beds and mattresses. Installing air conditioning is considered a social faux pas; dedicated fairgoers boast about their ability to withstand the heat. However, in the fair's newer nouveau riche neighborhoods—those cabins spreading in pine-and-oak groves

*U*nder the Tennessee state capitol, festival-goers fill Legislative Plaza in Nashville. Since the capitol was completed in the 1850s (it was designed by Philadelphia architect William Strickland, who is buried in the building), the steps and the grounds around it have been the center of Nashville government and commerce. It is used, as well, for social gatherings.

*C*lannish Southerners gather for games and other Scottish traditions at the Annual Highland Games and Gathering of the Clans at North Carolina's Grandfather Mountain. The grounds on the mountain seat several activities.

Few cities love a parade like New Orleans. And the best in the Crescent City is on Fat Tuesday, or Mardi Gras. Commerce takes a backseat to Mardi Gras festivities, in which at least sixty parades wind down New Orleans streets during the twelve-day event.

*T*he Neshoba County Fair near Philadelphia, Mississippi, celebrated its one-hundredth anniversary in 1989. Entire families live for a week at the fair in family-built cabins (some dating to the fair's earliest days). Along "streets," under tall oaks, beside the rim of a horse track, and angling around Founder's Square, 560 cabins house fairgoers.

*H*igh in the upcountry of South Carolina, friends and neighbors drop by for mountain music, 'long about sundown, every Saturday night at Cuzzins General Store, near Walhalla. Tourists at nearby state parks unlimber lawn chairs for the free concerts. Like gristmills, country stores served as a place to congregate and catch up on the latest community news.

*T*he front porch and grounds of Wakefield,
a plantation house near Saint Francisville,
Louisiana, serve as the site for a reunion of the
descendants of the home's builder, Lewis
Stirling. Front porches offer cool breezes and a
window to the world, and extend the first
greeting of Southern hospitality: "Y'all come on
up and sit a spell."

A bench and a shade tree provide the forum for passin' the time of day. In Center, Texas, the Shelby
County Courthouse functions like hundreds of others around the South—as a center for the town's
commercial, governmental, and social functions.

*F*rom setting sun to rising sun, pork barbecue cooks slowly in the hiss and smoke of oak and hickory chips. Preparations for a North Carolina "pig-pickin'" are an all-night affair. Cooks stay up the night tending the fire, turning the meat, and renewing friendships. Like the small-town barber shop, the outdoor barbecue kitchens remain largely an all-male domain.

Throngs of sun-worshipers, would-be sailors, and swimmers congregate at Wrightsville Beach, North Carolina, a seaside getaway.

Richmonders still gather at the Virginia state capitol at noon to meet with friends and spread brown-bag lunches on the grass or along the terraced brick walk. The parklike grounds feature statues of Virginia heroes. An iron fence, erected in 1819 to keep cattle and pigs off the grounds, edges the perimeter.

*H*orse racing's most celebrated event, the Kentucky Derby, is intensely Southern, from its Derby Day parties and mint juleps to the spires of the Churchill Downs grandstand. The Sport of Kings has deep Southern roots. Its American beginnings were in the South. Its aura fits well with the life-style—real or imagined—of the plantation aristocracy. And the region, especially Kentucky's famed Bluegrass, remains a favorite home to horse breeding.

The foxhound barrels across open farmland or lopes through pine forests. Either way, fox hunting brings a bit of European tradition to the Southern countryside. Red jackets flash. Horns blare. Beagles bay. And a place like Southern Pines, North Carolina, is filled with the excitement of the chase.

*T*he hunter waits. Whether in a duck blind in Stuttgart, Arkansas, or a deer stand in central Texas, the game is much the same. Out on the land, often camouflaged to appear a part of it, the hunter becomes a link in the ageless tradition that began when his forefathers took a living from what nature provided.

*T*he fisherman deals with two worlds. One is his own. He can outfit that with as many bass boats and fancy rods as he wants. But he still has to deal with a world he cannot see or control. Below the surface of the water, the world belongs to the fish. If he is lucky—or skillful—enough, the fisherman can reach from one to the other and emerge the victor.

On the fields of battle, the hope and glory of the South and the fate of the United States were sorely tested. The war scarred the land and split the nation, but it set a people free. In one of the nation's largest Civil War re-creations, present-day troops reenact the Battle of New Market, fought on May 15, 1864. To bolster the Confederate line's collapsing center, General J. C. Breckenridge committed 247 young cadets from nearby Virginia Military Institute with these words, "Put the boys in . . . and may God forgive me." Ten died.

*O*ver twenty-five million bricks form the massive Third System coastal fortification named after the Polish hero of the American Revolution. Fort Pulaski was built after the War of 1812 to protect the approach to Savannah from foreign invaders. Captured bloodlessly by Confederate forces early in the Civil War, the brick fort was to fall to Union rifled cannon on April 11, 1862.

*A*n all-too-familar sight at battlefields across the South, the endless rows of markers that recall the incredibly high cost of the War Between the States. The South, with a population of about nine million (including over three million slaves) suffered almost a half million casualties, including about 258,000 dead. The North, with a population of about twenty-one million, lost 359,528 dead with another 275,175 wounded.

In the bloodiest engagement of the Civil War, Lee's first invasion of the North was stopped in the battles of the Antietam campaign. This dirt road, known as Bloody Lane, was the scene of savage fighting on September 17, 1862.

After the Battle of Shiloh, fought near Pittsburg Landing on the Tennessee River in April 1862, the wounded of both armies crawled to this small pond to drink and wash their wounds. The water turned red from their blood.

The church of San Antonio de Valero mission is all that remains of the Alamo. Here, in 1836, Lieutenant Colonel Travis and his volunteers held out for two weeks against the army of Santa Anna. Their defeat became the rallying cry for Texas independence.

With Simmons Ridge as a formidable backdrop, the Bachelor Officers' Quarters at Fort Davis stands as a silent reminder of the dangers inherent in the westward expansion. Built in 1854 to protect the San Antonio to El Paso road from Comanche and Apache attack, the garrison was abandoned by Federal troops early in the Civil War. In 1867, the fort was reoccupied by six troops from the all-black Ninth Cavalry Regiment, the famous Buffalo Soldiers. Fort Davis was one of the largest forts in the West, with fifty-nine adobe buildings arranged formally around the parade ground.

Machines That Shaped The South

As the South, along with the rest of the world, moved from an agrarian society to a modern, industrialized one, it was technology that helped to move us and shape the ways we used the land.

As new technologies developed, the South adopted and adapted those technologies—sometimes with the reluctance of ignorance and apathy and sometimes with the fresh enthusiasm of a people who know that times must change.

The first settlers hugged the Southern seacoast with a tight embrace. The ocean was their physical and spiritual link with the Old World. Along the east coast, travel to the interior was limited by the fall line and the Appalachian Mountains.

Agriculture, a labor-intensive process, was made economically possible by the development of the plantation system and the institution of slavery. The development of the cotton gin late in the eighteenth century and the mechanization of the textile industry in England created a tremendous demand for cotton. Planters pushed west into what was to become Alabama and Mississippi in search of more land.

The development of steam power in England soon spread to the New World. By the second decade of the nineteenth century, steamboats were plying the Southern rivers. Faster and larger than the man-powered flatboats and keelboats that had been in use, the steam-powered boats speeded settlement of the interior South. With ready transportation, towns sprang up along the Mississippi, the Tennessee, the Alabama, the Arkansas, the Tombigbee, and the Chattahoochee.

Another new invention, the steam train, helped in this westward expansion. Horatio Allen's Best Friend of Charleston began the first scheduled railroad service on Christmas Day, 1830. By 1833, the line extended all the way to Hamburg, South Carolina, 136 miles from Charleston. Farther to the north, the Baltimore and Ohio Railroad, which had been chartered in 1827, operated its diminutive locomotive, Tom Thumb. By 1852, the tracks extended from Baltimore to Wheeling, then to Virginia. The South, indeed all of America, was gripped by railroad fever. By the eve of the Civil War, over ten thousand miles of railroad tracks veined much of the South, but not, as our Confederate generals were to discover, with the density of the lines in the North.

After the Civil War, the South, as well as the rest of the nation, continued to move west. New industries developed, and established ones grew to meet the increased demands for raw materials. The virgin yellow pine forests of Mississippi and Louisiana fell to the ax of a growing nation. In 1909, lumber production in the South peaked at sixteen billion board feet. By 1920, most of the virgin yellow pine was gone.

In search of cheap labor and to be close to the raw material, cotton textile manufacturing began to move from New England to the South after the Civil War. Soon red brick mills sprang up in the Piedmont region of North and South Carolina and Georgia. Mill villages were constructed for the influx of workers, most of whom came from the subsistence farms of Appalachia. For many poor whites, the job in the mill and the life in the mill town were their first urban experiences. In an era before child labor laws, girls and boys often began work before age ten, sometimes starting as young as four. Working conditions were poor; long hours, cotton dust, and the noise of the machinery aged children before their time. Pay was low, often only two or three dollars a week.

During this same period, two other industries—coal mining and steel making—emerged in the Appalachian South. As in the textile mills, work in the mines and steel mills was hard and dangerous. For many young boys, schooling ended after a few grades, as they joined their fathers and older brothers in the mines and mills. Home was often a company-owned house; food and clothing came from the company store. Whole cities, such as Birmingham, grew up around the steel mills.

The industrialization of the South went hand in hand with its urbanization. European immigrants, emancipated slaves, and rural whites flooded into the cities of the region in the years following the Civil War. The invention of the streetcar, trolley, and later, the automobile allowed the cities to spread out over the landscape as new suburbs grew.

On the farm, developments in agriculture increased productivity and lessened the need for a large population of farm workers. For example, the diversification from a single-crop (specifically cotton) economy allowed the planting of crops such as soybeans that required only a twentieth of the labor to produce. Irrigation allowed profitable farm production to push into the more arid parts of the Southwest. And, most importantly, the mechanization of the farm further reduced the need for manual labor. Accelerated by the Second World War, tractors replaced mules and the old sharecropper system. In 1940, 43.1 percent of the South's population lived on farms; by 1970, only 6.9 percent.

World War II brought a flood of Federal money into the region as military bases were built to take advantage of the South's mild winters for year-round training. Defense plants followed in search of a ready supply of workers. For a South still struggling with the Depression, the war brought a hitherto unknown level of prosperity. Per capita income doubled as the region reached full employment. Billions of dollars flowed into the South for construction of factories, shipyards, and training fields. Quiet villages grew at a boomtown pace. The population of Pascagoula, Mississippi, rapidly increased from six thousand to over thirty thousand as workers came off the farms to work at the new Ingalls shipyard. In rural east Tennessee, the super-secret work on the Manhattan Project created the new city of Oak Ridge virtually overnight. By the time its product was dropped on Hiroshima in August of 1945, the city had a population of over seventy-five thousand.

After the Second World War, the development of the mechanical cotton picker launched another migration of farm workers into the city. And along with the introduction of air conditioning, which helped to mitigate the heat and humidity of the Southern summer, came a flood of immigrants from the North. Attracted by nonunion labor and less expensive land costs, factories, too, moved south.

As the region's labor force becomes better educated, this trend is continuing with white-collar industries. The development of electronic communications has allowed companies to move from the major trade centers of the Northeast to the South. Technological incubators such as North Carolina's Research Triangle Park have helped attract both business and skilled workers to the region. Climate, geography, and political pull have brought some of the most advanced technologies, such as the space program, to the South.

—Louis Joyner

*G*eorge Washington chose Harpers Ferry, located at the juncture of the Shenandoah and Potomac rivers, as the site for an armory to manufacture muskets. Powered by the rapidly flowing water, the armory had produced over a half million muskets and rifles by the start of the Civil War. An 1859 raid by fanatical abolitionist John Brown, in an attempt to obtain arms for a slave rebellion, was quelled by Marines led by Robert E. Lee.

*I*n the years before steam, power for industry came from the action of falling water. Gristmills, such as this one on Glade Creek in West Virginia, ground corn and wheat for early settlers. Along the fall line, larger mills were developed to use water power to drive looms for weaving cloth and to power machine tools.

*T*he development of the steam engine and the shallow-draft paddle wheel boat opened the interior South to settlement. Easy transportation of the major crop—cotton—allowed the rapid growth of cities such as Memphis, Vicksburg, Natchez, and Baton Rouge along the Mississippi River, as well as other cities along the region's smaller rivers.

As the web of rails spread across the South and the nation, railroad stations, like this Baltimore & Ohio station in Point of Rocks, Maryland, became the community's link with the outside world. The trains brought goods and visitors, while the clicking telegraph key relayed news.

Standing now as a reminder of the South's industrial past, the Sloss-Sheffield Steel & Iron Company once produced four hundred tons of pig iron a day. The furnaces began production in 1882 at the site just east of downtown Birmingham. The furnace, which ceased operation in 1971, is now a museum to the industry that created the city.

Rising above the marshes, the shuttle awaits its mission. The Kennedy Space Center on Merritt Island, a few miles west of Cape Canaveral, has been the starting point for journeys to the moon, Mars, and beyond. The huge Saturn V rocket engines for the Apollo moon mission were developed and tested at Huntsville, Alabama's, Marshall Space Flight Center. The Johnson Space Center in Houston controlled the missions.

Great Resorts, Grand Hotels

From Virginia's warm mineral springs to the cool breezes on Florida's Gulf Coast, Southerners have gathered for two centuries at spas, hotels, and lush resorts.

In Southern cities, hotels—gleaming new high-rises with soaring atriums or venerable old inns perfectly restored—offer more than a room for the night. Guests may shop boutiques, work out in fitness centers, tour an art collection, browse a library, dine, or dance. Many guests are there to work, and hotels offer executive floors with computer terminals and facsimile machines to speed on-the-road work.

City dwellers go to resorts to play, enticed by the golf, tennis, skiing, sunbathing, and scenery. High in mountains or rising among dunes, resorts are rooms with a view, a combination of lodging and nature where scenery is part of the package price.

In the South, our climate spurs the growth of resorts. We can boast of some of the nation's first. And from one city to another, hotels stand as symbols of their locales.

Legend has signed many guest registers at city hotels in the South. We are fortunate that both the stories and the structures survive.

From the balcony of the Mills House in Charleston, Robert E. Lee watched the conflagration that swept much of the city in 1861.

The manager of The Galt House in Louisville asked guest Charles Dickens if he needed anything. "When I need you, landlord, I'll ring for you," snapped the famous English novelist, who soon found himself out on the street.

The Driskill Hotel in Austin is just down the street from the state capitol. Once, it was said, the Texas legislature had three houses—the senate, the house of representatives, and the Driskill Hotel.

One day at The Peabody in Memphis, as a practical joke, duck hunters tossed their live decoys into the lobby's marble fountain. A tradition was launched.

Often the distinctive feature of a city's skyline, grand hotels in the South have always been the places to go for top-of-the-line accommodations. As our downtowns flourished, then sagged in the middle of this century, so did many of the grand hotels. But several were beautifully restored and stand as proud monuments of tradition and renewal.

The great events of private lives—debutante balls, wedding feasts, honeymoons—were staged at city hotels until those establishments became cherished landmarks, places in the heart of a community. Memphis felt deeply the loss of The Peabody when it closed in the mid-1970s and was overjoyed when it returned a few years and a twenty-one-million-dollar renovation later. "I actually saw tears of joy when some Memphians came into the lobby when the hotel reopened," said a hotel spokesman.

Its traditions were restored, too. The ducks came back. Each day, to the accompaniment of a taped narrative and lively march, they waddle out of an elevator and promenade down a red carpet to the fountain. On the top floor, big band music has returned to the Skyway room, where Glenn Miller, Tommy Dorsey, and others played. Sunset dances once again end days on the Plantation Roof.

Old hotels in other cities rise in restored grandeur: The Seelbach/Doubletree in Louisville; the Hermitage Hotel in Nashville; the Eola in Natchez; the Jefferson Sheraton in Richmond; the Capital Hotel in Little Rock. The Adolphus Hotel, built by beer baron Adolphus Busch in 1912, is dwarfed today by much taller, newer structures. Yet, the baroque-style building still stands as one of the city's most recognizable buildings.

New hotels in several cities also speak of place. In Atlanta in the 1960s and 1970s, the blue bubble of the Hyatt Regency and the round spire of the Westin Peachtree Plaza arose as landmarks that identified the downtown skyline. The Stouffer's Winston Plaza in Winston-Salem captures the city's long love affair with art. Some eight hundred works of art are on display, in a city that boasts more than twenty galleries and museums.

In Birmingham, the old Hotel Tutwiler was demolished in 1974. But a new one has arisen with the same name, and its design, service, and cuisine reflect a new, brighter image of the city built by steel mills.

Some urban establishments blur the distinction between city hotel and resort retreat. Certainly Orlando's Hyatt Regency Grand Cypress, in the central Florida playground, plays both roles. Business people gather for meetings and conferences. Yet outside the hotel doors spreads a half-acre blue lagoon with tropical vegetation and cascading waterfalls. Trolleys take guests to the Jack Nicklaus-designed golf course, tennis courts, a lakeside beach, and jogging and nature trails.

Early in their history, Southerners took time off from building the country to soothe their souls at resorts. Indians led us to the first ones; in the late eighteenth and early nineteenth centuries, settlers followed the examples of Native Americans and sought out the waters of warm springs. By the mid-1800s, at springs resorts such as The Greenbrier in White Sulphur Springs, West Virginia, and The Homestead in Hot Springs, Virginia, Southerners "took the baths" for their health. Their visit was also social. Balls, gambling, great dining, and music highlighted the season where the South's elite rubbed elbows.

Fitness and health have always been the draw for us to spend a few days in paradise. In the late 1800s, just as now, a health consciousness drew visitors to resorts to drink the waters from chalybeate springs and seek out towns supposedly infused with clean air. The climate of certain Southern towns was considered healthy for specific ailments. Consumptives, for example, came to The Grove Park Inn in Asheville, North Carolina.

They also chose Pinehurst, in the sandhills of North Carolina, where, in the late 1800s, a game helped reshape the design of resorts. To complement the manicured layout of golf courses, sprawling land and facilities were needed. Frederick Law Olmsted was called to design a village with cottages, a hotel, shops, and a meetinghouse/chapel. Pinehurst arose as a community as well as a resort.

The Jekyll Island Club on the Georgia coast was built as a winter "town" for the very, very rich. From the late 1800s until World War II, names like Rockefeller, Gould, Morgan, and Pulitzer graced the registers at the clubhouse. They built expansive "cottages," hunted, fished, picnicked, played golf and tennis. Kate Brown, a tutor, described them as "a rare collection of very high bred and exclusive animals, perfectly useless to society but enjoying their gilded cage very much."

Railroads also built resorts. Henry Flagler constructed a railroad along the

Atlantic coast in Florida, and a string of resorts from St. Augustine to Miami. On the other side, Henry Plant built grand resorts in such places as Tampa and Boca Raton. Many of those hotels stand as monuments to the tourism industry they spawned. The Spanish styles of architect Addison Mizner in what is now Boca Raton Golf and Country Club speak of an entire era in Florida.

The great Florida resorts such as The Breakers in Palm Beach, the Don CeSar near St. Petersburg, and the Biltmore in Coral Gables, opened their doors to the very rich. But where the rich went, the middle class would scrimp and save and surely follow.

They would change the face of resorts after World War II. Pinehurst was the harbinger of things to come in the form and functions of resorts for the middle class. Along seacoasts and nestled into mountains, resorts were designed as "livable" environments, where visitors would come to spend a weekend, a season, or the rest of their lives.

As prominent as Pinehurst in resort development, Sea Pines Plantation on Hilton Head Island, South Carolina, turned another corner. In the mid-1960s, the young developer Charles E. Fraser initiated a new trend by subjugating construction to natural beauty, blending vacation structures with their surroundings, and using quiet colors of gray and gray-green cypress as the main building material to match the sea island forests.

Following the Sea Pines Plantation example, many other resorts walked softly on the fragile environment. They stilted boardwalks above dunes, attached strict building codes, and left portions of their property in its natural state. One resort, Callaway Gardens in Pine Mountain, Georgia, was built as a caretaker of the land. The Callaway family nourished twenty-five hundred acres of eroded cotton fields into a lush paradise of native and introduced flora. Around these gardens, resort facilities were built. Now, visitors arrive to see spring's show and tour botanical conservatories and listen to silent flights in a butterfly house. They also come to settle into an inn or a condominium, play golf and tennis, fish, and walk and bicycle along woodland paths. The resort serves as a backdrop to the natural beauty. In fact, the resort is owned by the nonprofit Ida Cason Callaway Memorial Foundation, a company established to further education and research in the natural sciences.

To a large measure, resorts have taught us to restore old neighborhoods or build new communities focusing on the relationship between design and environment. Nowhere better is that expressed than at Seaside, a new resort community near Destin, Florida. Detailed planning and zoning codes require and encourage certain aspects of Southern vernacular architecture. Washed in pastel colors and gleaming with metal roofs, the community features breezy porches, white latticework, and playful gazebos behind the roll of dunes. Seaside is reminiscent of our oldest resorts, yet designed with an eye for the future.

—Gary D. Ford

*S*ome of the first guests at the Homestead arrived by horse and buggy. Built around hot mineral springs, this eighteenth-century spa was one of America's first resorts.

*T*he air around Asheville, North Carolina, was good for what ailed you. Or so thought many who came to resorts like The Grove Park Inn in the early 1900s, when a health trend was sweeping the country.

In the sandhills of central North Carolina, Frederick Law Olmsted's Pinehurst set standards for today's resort layouts. Around a golf course, he spread a hotel, village, shops, and a church/community meetinghouse.

"The Mississippi Delta begins in the lobby of The Peabody, and ends on Catfish Row in Vicksburg." So went the saying about this grand hotel room. It was restored in detail, right down to the ducks in the fountain, in the late 1970s.

*M*any grand city hotels date from the turn of the century, and most have been lavishly restored in recent years. The Adolphus, although now dwarfed by the Dallas skyline, still stands high as a symbol of the city.

The very rich once wintered at their Jekyll Island Club in Georgia—hunting, fishing, and playing golf, tennis, and croquet. Few of their "cottages" contained kitchens. They dined at their clubhouse, now a beautifully restored hotel.

Henry Flagler built several resort hotels along his railroad in the late 1890s. One of the greatest on the Florida Atlantic coast is The Breakers in Palm Beach. Built in the Italian Renaissance style in 1925, it replaced an earlier structure.

*T*he Red Fox Tavern sits in the center of historic Middleburg, the heart of Virginia's fox hunting country. The tavern began life as Chinn's Ordinary in 1728. Well into its second century, it saw the ravages of the Civil War as the downstairs was turned into an infirmary for Confederate wounded. The bar in the dining room was made from the field operating table used by the army surgeon who served with General Jeb Stuart's cavalry. Today the dining room is a favorite gathering place for local residents as well as guests.

*S*panish and Moorish styles were in vogue around the 1920s when resorts like The Cloister on Sea Island, Georgia, and others farther south in Florida were rising. Consistently one of America's highest-rated resorts, The Cloister was built in 1928.

*W*alt Disney World's Grand Floridian Hotel is reminiscent of Victorian-era Florida. Steeped in comfortable elegance, the Grand Floridian, which opened in 1988, is the first resort of its kind to be built since the turn of the century.

*R*ising at the edge of the gulf in Galveston, the Galvez Hotel has stood since 1911, when excursion trains brought bathers to its doors from across the Southwest.

*H*arbour Town forms the centerpiece of Sea Pines Plantation on Hilton Head Island. Charles Fraser designed the resort community to blend quietly with the surrounding island forest. His subdued, gentle style began a trend in resort design that is still widely copied, even in nonresort communities.

The Tie That Binds

Home. Homeplace. The old homeplace. In the South, such simple words evoke the strongest of emotions, the deepest and earliest of memories.

Here, where we are rooted to the land by ancestry and collective memory, home often translates into specific structures. Many of us are still tied, by invisible cords as strong as steel, to a house, to a homeplace. In this house-proud region of a house-proud nation, a family's residence represents to the world those most sacrosanct of all human ties.

Sometimes the houses we have built have been intensely individualistic, sometimes mannered and carefully wrought; always they have been built with roots and pride. Each house that survives for a span of years has many stories to tell, the whys and hows that molded often simple building materials into more than the sum of their parts. Indeed the charm of such an evolving house, added to over time, is so great that today architects consciously design new houses to emulate instantly both the evolving design and the patina of age.

The South's earliest houses, however, were built without such self-consciousness. These houses were shelter for the first settlers—in the English colony of Virginia, in Spanish Florida, and in the French settlements along the Mississippi River and Gulf Coast. Later, more substantial houses, with roots to the Old World, were built by representatives of

the Colonial governments and by those amassing their fortunes. The earliest surviving Southern house is the sturdy, workmanlike, brick Adam Thoroughgood house, which was built by the prosperous former indentured servant in Virginia in 1636.

The restlessness of pioneers, the search for land, and new immigrants drove the frontier west. Log houses generally marked the distinction between civilization and the frontier. If the frontier settlers planned to stay in one place for any length of time, they carefully hewed the logs into sturdy houses. Later in the nineteenth century, with the arrival of sawmills and railroads, many of the log houses were sided over with milled boards. The same pattern of building—early log houses, often sided over—was repeated as settlers pushed south and west across the Appalachians to the Mississippi River and into Arkansas and east Texas.

A notch above the log house was the linear plan that became known as the I-house. Because these houses were often built by the first planters in a region—from the Tidewater to the west and south—they are frequently referred to as plantation plain houses. A common early plan for this style was composed of four rooms—two downstairs and two upstairs. Later, a center hall might have been added, an adaptation of the prevailing Georgian style. As early as the late eighteenth century, full-width, shed-roof porches became a hallmark feature of the I-house in the South.

The center hall is important in the study of Southern architecture, with origins sometimes shrouded both in legend and history. The center hall arrangement in grand houses is usually attributed to an adaptation of the English Georgian manor house plan. In the subtropical Deep South, the hall through the house was typically wide, with doors at the ends for cross ventilation. Some architectural historians now suggest that this room arrangement was influenced by simple log houses, as well. In hot climates, these houses consisted of two rooms (or pens) connected by a covered breezeway (or dogtrot). The origins of the I-house and the center hall notwithstanding, local carpenters continued to build in that basic style well into the twentieth century.

Although most early settlers lived in modest structures, land-rich planters built much more substantial houses on the banks of the major rivers from Virginia through the Carolinas. Along these waterways, well before the American Revolution, planters amassed vast holdings to grow tobacco and indigo, the first of our Southern export crops. The early Georgian-style plantation houses that they built were typically sited to face the river, the route both for people and crops to the outside world.

That these houses so closely resembled those being built across the Atlantic was not an accident. The educated elite had libraries containing architectural treatises, as well as more prosaic architectural pattern books. For example, historians know that Thomas Jefferson referred to specific books, including Andrea Palladio's *The Four Books of Architecture*, for the first designs of Monticello.

The fact that Palladio, a sixteenth-century Italian architect, had such a pronounced effect on a young, raw land is not as surprising as it may seem. In the older colonies, the first great houses tended to reflect the British heritage, as well as Britain's interpretation of Palladio. Some theories of architecture and history conclude that his designs, first done for landed Italians, were translated directly to Britain's first colony of Ireland, to the West Indies, and to the mainland of the new world. By the late seventeenth century, both the labor-intensive plantation system and Palladio's theories of proportion and scale were comfortably settled in the Southern colonies.

This feel for appropriate plantation manor design moved easily ashore as slave revolts and malaria drove sugar planters, particularly those of French descent, to relocate along the incredibly fertile lower Mississippi River. Later waves of planters came overland from the older states, bringing the cotton culture to the upland delta and river bottoms of the Deep South. While only a small fraction of the population lived in the mansions built between 1825 and the outbreak of the Civil War, these houses have come to epitomize the South in myth and legend.

At the same time, urbanism and urban housing were evident in the states of the Old South even before the American Revolution. In Virginia, Williamsburg became the seat of government, and the Governor's Palace set architectural standards for grand houses. Likewise, the simple Georgian cottages of artisans have been copied to this day. The early seacoast trading centers of Annapolis, Charleston, and Savannah developed their own styles of city houses. Among the best known are the Charleston single and double houses, named for their narrow designs and shady side piazzas. From the late eighteenth century well into the nineteenth century, Annapolis row houses, Savannah high-stooped houses, and New Orleans shotgun houses adapted stylish architectural features to their distinctive, urban house styles.

As these urban and social centers grew, architecture changed. After the Revolutionary War, the Georgian style in America began evolving into a related style known as Federal. The change in name signifies the break with the mother country. Such a break was basically in name only. Today, architectural historians say that the boxy, symmetrical Federal style is more precisely the American version of the English Adam style (named for the English architect Robert Adam and his brothers). As settlers moved inland, the more prosperous took the style with them as far west as the Mississippi River.

Although the Adam style is closely associated with the early years of the new nation, another style which had a

As the South changed dramatically in the postwar years, so did the concepts of housing. Millions of housing units were built across the United States for returning servicemen with their low-interest home loans. Street after street, suburb after suburb sprang up with houses that differed little from those built in Illinois and California. The same style of house was likely to be built in Birmingham and Burbank, Atlanta and Anaheim, New Orleans and Newark. By the 1950s, the common house was the standard ranch style, which was often unsuitable for the hot Southern climate.

The suburbanization of the South, a trend in the 1950s, accelerated into the 1960s with disturbing consequences. As families moved to outlying suburbs and subdivisions, neighborhoods of row houses, single houses, bungalows, shotguns, and Queen Annes deteriorated. The more substantial houses were often divided into apartments or rooming houses. Close-in neighborhoods of some of the oldest and proudest Southern cities became slums. Even in smaller towns, urbanization, highway widening, and the loss of a sense of history meant the demise of many landmark houses.

Beginning in the 1970s, the preservation movement, which began in the South, spurred the rejuvenation of many neighborhoods. Again, it became fashionable to live in the city, to walk to work, to appreciate history. Across the South, young families and professional people began to move back. And block by block, whole neighborhoods were made livable again. The same trends continued, too, in small towns and rural areas, where older houses were in demand for family living.

Even at the height of the internationalist and modernist architectural movements, some Southern architects continued to design traditional houses, rooted in classic designs of the past. In the late 1970s and early 1980s, these masters of Southern architecture saw increased interest in their work—often from younger families seeking the stability of tradition. At the same time, young architects were rediscovering and at times reinterpreting the past. In a movement called regionalism, they were designing vernacular houses geared to the climates and life-styles of the South. Again, we recognized why we need steeply pitched roofs, wide overhangs, floor-length windows, operable shutters, front porches, cross ventilation. We had come home.

—Linda Hallam

Arguably the most famous house in the South, Mount Vernon was saved from ruin by early preservationists in 1858. George Washington inherited his 1½-story, four-room house on a bank high above the Potomac River, in 1761. Before he married, he had the house raised to 2½ stories and redecorated. Though the house appears to be stone, it is wood planking which has been rusticated to give the appearance of blocks. Washington continued to make improvements to the house while he led the American forces during the Revolution. He retired to Mount Vernon and died there in 1799.

The first permanent residences in the early
Colonial settlements were built in the late
Medieval styles of England and Europe. The
brick Newbold-White House, believed to be the
oldest house in North Carolina, has the end
chimneys and fortress appearance that were
hallmarks of pre-1700s construction. The house
was constructed around 1685 near Hertford, an
early town on the banks of the Perquimans River.

*T*ennessee's first governor, John Sevier, spent his last years at his Marble Springs farm near Knoxville. Built of squared logs, the two-room cabin illustrates the simple but sturdy structures of the first wave of pioneers. Typically one room (known as a pen) would have been built first for shelter, then a second added. The stacked stone fireplace provided fire for cooking and heat. Today, the early log house is part of the John Sevier Historic Site.

*P*lantation plain houses, sometimes called I-houses, were often the first substantial structures to replace rough log shelters. Based on a British folk form settlers brought to North America, the houses are traditionally two rooms wide and one room deep. By the late eighteenth century, shed-roof porches usually shaded houses, such as this restored North Carolina farmhouse.

*C*losely associated with Southern history, the Stone House at today's Manassas National Battlefield Park survived two pivotal battles of the Civil War. The Georgian-style house, constructed of Virginia fieldstone, was originally constructed as an inn that served travelers along the Warrenton Turnpike. During the Civil War, the building was used as a field hospital in battles known as First and Second Bull Run.

*C*onsidered by many architectural historians as the finest Colonial Georgian-Palladian house ever built, Drayton Hall, near Charleston, is one of the few surviving grand rice and cotton plantations along the Ashley River. Construction started with slave-made bricks in the late 1730s, and the house was occupied by John Drayton by 1742. The Draytons were the only family to ever occupy the house, which was purchased by the National Trust for Historic Preservation in 1974. Because Drayton Hall was used only as a country retreat from the 1870s, it has never been modernized. Most of the interiors were painted only twice, the last time in 1885.

Near Richmond, Virginia, Tuckahoe Plantation is considered by architectural historians to be one of the country's finest examples of the eighteenth-century plantation house. The influence of English Georgian architecture is apparent in the boxy design and pediment entry. The wood frame house is still surrounded by eighteenth-century outbuildings.

*W*illiam Byrd II, founder of Richmond, constructed Westover on the James River about 1730. The Byrds were one of the first Southern families to found fortunes on the land. This early example of Colonial Georgian architecture reflects the manor house style then in vogue in England. It was also indicative of the great houses that were built as the plantation economy spread south and west.

Thomas Jefferson originally based his design of Monticello on the works of the sixteenth-century Italian architect Andrea Palladio and on available architecture books. After representing the young United States in Paris for five years, Jefferson returned to his Virginia mountaintop to redesign the house in the new Classical Revival style. Historians now trace the Classical Revival style to the early nineteenth-century interest in Greece and Rome. At the same time, this early Classical Revival was the forerunner of the much more widespread Greek Revival. Jefferson worked with the design and redesign of Monticello for forty years. Today, the house stands as evidence of his enduring genius.

*A*ndrew Jackson's beloved wife, Rachel, chose the spot for The Hermitage, built on a thousand-acre farm near Nashville between 1819 and 1821. The original center hall plan, with two full stories, was typical of the brick houses prosperous farmers and planters built in the early decades of the nineteenth century. After a fire in 1834, Jackson modernized the house with fashionable Greek Revival details. He retired to The Hermitage in 1837 and died there in 1845. Today, the ancient sugar maples turn the grounds, where the Jacksons are buried, into a blaze of color every autumn. The carefully preserved house and grounds are now a house museum open to the public.

*O*akley Plantation House, in wooded, gently rolling West Feliciana Parish, near St. Francisville, Louisiana, is associated with artist John James Audubon. During a four-month stay in 1821 as a tutor in drawing, Audubon created thirty-two of his famous bird paintings. Built in 1799, Oakley is a fine example of the West Indies-influenced Louisiana plantation house adapted to the subtropical climate. Louvered galleries allow for ventilation but keep out the rain and glare.

*T*he oldest wooden structure in Louisiana, Magnolia Mound is now in the center of Baton Rouge. Between 1791 and 1798, the French raised cottage was built for the overseer of wealthy landowner John Joyce. The house is a notable example of early construction as the thick walls are packed with bousillage, a mixture of mud, Spanish moss, and animal hair. Also typical of the period, rooms are built side by side without corridors. Magnolia Mound is a house museum, open throughout the year.

*B*uilt in 1857, the Manship House in Jackson, Mississippi, is a fine Southern example of the Gothic Revival style. Such romantic house styles, popularized by Andrew Jackson Downing, were a reaction to the formality of the earlier decades of the nineteenth century. The centered gable, decorated with vergeboard, was a hallmark of Gothic Revival. The Manship's house-centered gable extends forward to form a covered entrance. The house is open to the public.

A Moving Landscape

Roads and highways connect one place to another, but the road itself constitutes a primary and profound experience of landscape. The future of the South's sense of itself is bound, for better or worse, with the quality of these lines across the land.

They are called by names or numbers, sometimes both. Lanes. County Roads. State Highways. Interstates. Parkways. Expressways. In Texas, many hundreds of thousands of miles of two-lane gravel or blacktop are designated FM, farm-to-market. In Tennessee, they are often called pikes. As in Granny White Pike.

The utility of getting from place to place is what most often comes uppermost, and "improvements" always mean straightening or widening. But the road is also landscape. It is the way we experience the landscape most of the time. Roads and highways can be part of the landscape, or they can soar above it as the new superhighways often do. But wider is not necessarily better when this aspect of the road is considered. The narrow old road slipping gently through a rural scene, no shoulders, the grass right there at the edge, the next movement dictated by the lay of the land rather than an engineer's smooth calculation, may be a much more satisfying experience than an efficient but boring new road.

The leading writer on the landscape in America, J. B. Jackson, wrote in *The Necessity for Ruins, and Other Topics*: "The building of roads . . . is now the most powerful force for the destruction or creation of landscapes that we have."

Many of the most landscape-sensitive roads the South has are inherited from a time when, either by instinct or by necessity, the routing and construction of them worked to the setting. But, then, some of the region's most appealing drives have been constructed during the past several decades. The great Blue Ridge Parkway, a collaboration between landscape architects and engineers begun during the Great Depression as a linear national park, is one. And many stretches of interstate highway were planned and built to respond to the landscape they pass through. If they have not been degraded with billboards, these highways offer beautiful and lasting impressions of the South's landscape.

When the landscape itself—notably, the canopy of trees growing along the road—arches over the road, it produces a thrilling architecture. The coastal zones of the South are noted for these experiences. When the road is part of a domesticated rural scene, as happens in the

Carolinas or Virginia or Tennessee with frequency, it becomes a shifting line that helps organize a painterly perspective. And when the roads are lined with fences for miles, as in the Kentucky Bluegrass—rising and falling and turning with slopes and boundary lines—the effect is nearly musical.

The road as medium, as our primary way to see and experience the beloved landscape of the South, has been taken for granted. For thousands of miles more each year, its precious edges are wasted by random development, signs, auto graveyards, and every sad use known to man. The loss is beginning to be registered. Some states, like North Carolina, are beginning to seriously designate, and seek protection for, scenic byways. A new interstate being built through the middle of Louisiana has been declared off-limits to billboards by the governor. In Tallahassee, Florida, five Canopy Roads leading into the city are preserved by ordinance, just as buildings are.

It is becoming clear, maybe too late in many places: the road *is* the landscape. It deserves protection as a cultural resource. Lose the road, lose the landscape.

—Philip Morris

Working its way through a rural landscape at Cape Hatteras, North Carolina, this road is the essence of local. The experience of moving along the road through woods, opening onto a meadow crowned by a church, crossing a creek, turning past houses: this is more than just transportation. It is the art of the landscape realized through the medium of the road.

101 left: Outer Banks, North Carolina/*Geoffrey Gilbert*

right: Four Holes Swamp, Francis Beidler Forest, Harleyville, South Carolina/*Beth Maynor*

102 Honey Creek, Fredericksburg, Texas/*Beth Maynor*

104 Padre Island, Texas/*Kimberly Parsons*

105 Gulf of Mexico/*Mike Clemmer*

106 Annapolis, Maryland/*John O'Hagan*

107 Reelfoot Lake, Lake and Obion Counties, Tennessee/*Bruce Roberts*

108 Mountain Creek Lake, Callaway Gardens, Pine Mountain, Georgia/*Sylvia Martin*

109 The Great Smoky Mountains, North Carolina/*Sylvia Martin*

110 Cumberland Island, Georgia/*Bruce Roberts*

111 Mexico Beach, Florida/*Geoffrey Gilbert*

Good Times Down Home

112 Fair Park, Dallas, Texas/*Kim Appel*

116 Legislative Plaza, Nashville, Tennessee/*Courtesy: State of Tennessee*

117 left: Grandfather Mountain, North Carolina/*Bruce Roberts*

right: New Orleans, Louisiana/*Frederica Georgia*

118 Neshoba County Fair, near Philadelphia, Mississippi/*Bruce Roberts*

119 Cuzzins General Store, near Walhalla, South Carolina/*Bruce Roberts*

120 left: Wakefield Plantation, near Saint Francisville, Louisiana/*Bruce Roberts*

right: Shelby County Courthouse, Center, Texas/*Frederica Georgia*

121 Franklinville, North Carolina/*Charles Walton IV*

122 Wrightsville Beach, North Carolina/*Mike Clemmer*

123 Virginia State Capitol, Richmond, Virginia/*Geoffrey Gilbert*

For The Sport Of It

124 Annapolis, Maryland/*Charles Walton IV*

126 top: University of Oklahoma, Norman, Oklahoma/*Kimberly Parsons*

bottom: Florida/*Geoffrey Gilbert*

127 Augusta, Georgia/*Van Chaplin*

129 Churchill Downs, Louisville, Kentucky/*Charles Walton IV*

130 Moore County Hounds Hunter Trials, Southern Pines, North Carolina/*Bruce Roberts*

131 top: Stuttgart, Arkansas/*Kim Appel*

bottom: Lake Seminole, Georgia/*Bruce Roberts*

Fields Of Glory

132 Fort Pulaski, Cockspur Island, Georgia/*Louis Joyner*

134 New Market, Virginia/*Bruce Roberts*

135 New Market Battlefield Park, New Market, Virginia/*Bruce Roberts*

136 Fort Pulaski, Cockspur Island, Georgia/*Louis Joyner*

137 Vicksburg, Mississippi

138 Bloody Lane, Antietam National Battlefield, Sharpsburg, Maryland/*Gary Clark*

139 The Bloody Pond, near Corinth, Mississippi/*Bruce Roberts*

140 The Alamo, San Antonio, Texas/*Kimberly Parsons*

141 Fort Davis, Davis Mountains, Texas/*Geoffrey Gilbert*

Machines That Shaped The South

142 Replica of the Best Friend of Charleston steam passenger train, Train Depot Museum, Branchville, South Carolina/*John O'Hagan*

144 Harpers Ferry, West Virginia/*Mac Jamieson*

145 Glade Creek Grist Mill, Babcock State Park, near Thurmond, West Virginia/*Mike Clemmer*

146 Delta Queen, Mississippi River, New Orleans, Louisiana/*Bruce Roberts*

147 Baltimore & Ohio Railroad Station, Point of Rocks, Maryland/*Geoffrey Gilbert*

148 Sloss Furnaces, Birmingham, Alabama/*Kim Appel*

149 John F. Kennedy Space Center, Merritt Island, Florida/*Gary Clark*

Great Resorts, Grand Hotels

150 The Cloister, Sea Island, Georgia/*Sylvia Martin*

152 The Homestead, Hot Springs, Virginia/*Bruce Roberts*

153 Grove Park Inn, Asheville, North Carolina/*Bruce Roberts*

154 top: Pinehurst, North Carolina/*Bruce Roberts*

bottom: The Peabody, Memphis, Tennessee/*Louis Joyner*

155 The Adolphus, Dallas, Texas/*Frederica Georgia*

156 left: The Jekyll Island Club, Jekyll Island, Georgia/*Kim Appel*

right: The Breakers, Palm Beach, Florida/*Bruce Roberts*

157 Red Fox Tavern, Middleburg, Virginia/*Mike Clemmer*

158 left: The Cloister, Sea Island, Georgia/*Sylvia Martin*

right: Grand Floridian, Orlando, Florida

160 Galvez Hotel, Galveston, Texas/*Bruce Roberts*

161 Harbour Town, South Carolina/*Bruce Roberts*

The Tie That Binds

162 Charleston, South Carolina/*John O'Hagan*

167 Mount Vernon, Fairfax County, Virginia/*Mac Jamieson*

168 Newbold-White House, near Hertford, North Carolina/*Geoffrey Gilbert*

169 Marble Springs Farm, John Sevier Historic Site, near Knoxville, Tennessee

170 top: Rural North Carolina/*John O'Hagan*

bottom: Stone House, Manassas National Battlefield Park/*Dianne Young*

171 Drayton Hall, near Charleston, South Carolina/*Kim Appel*

172 Tuckahoe Plantation, near Richmond, Virginia/*Van Chaplin*

173 Westover Plantation, along the James River, Virginia/*Bruce Roberts*

174 Monticello, Charlottesville, Virginia/*John O'Hagan*

175 The Hermitage, near Nashville, Tennessee/*Bruce Roberts*

176 Charleston, South Carolina/*John O'Hagan*

177 top: Hope Plantation, near Windsor, North Carolina/*Bob Lancaster*

bottom: Oak Alley, near New Orleans, Louisiana/*Frederica Georgia*

178 Oakley Plantation House, near St. Francisville, Louisiana/*Mac Jamieson*

179 left: Magnolia Mound, Baton Rouge, Louisiana/*Frederica Georgia*

right: Manship House, Jackson, Mississippi/*John O'Hagan*

180 top: Steves Homestead, King William Historic District, San Antonio, Texas/*Mac Jamieson*

bottom: Longwood, near Natchez, Mississippi/*Van Chaplin*

181 Swan House, Atlanta, Georgia/*Howard L. Puckett*

A Moving Landscape

182 Shelby County, Alabama/*Beth Maynor*

183 Cape Hatteras, North Carolina/*Geoffrey Gilbert*

184 Maritime Forest, Cumberland Island, Georgia/*Geoffrey Gilbert*

185 Hill Country, Texas/*Kimberly Parsons*

186 Blue Ridge Parkway, Virginia-North Carolina Border/*Bruce Roberts*

188 Atchafalaya River Basin, Louisiana/*Kimberly Parsons*

189 top: Queens Road West, Charlotte, North Carolina/*Bruce Roberts*

bottom: Bowling Green, Kentucky/*Kim Appel*

jacket: Matagorda Island, Texas/Bruce Roberts
inset: The Old Rice Mill at Middleton Place, near Charleston, South Carolina/Sylvia Martin

SOUTHERN PLACES

A Classic Collection of W O R D S & I M A G E S

Designed by Cynthia Rose Cooper

Color separations by Capitol Engraving Company,
Nashville, Tennessee

Printed and bound by Arcata Graphics,
Kingsport, Tennessee

Text sheets are Sterling Litho Gloss
Westvāco,
New York, New York

Endleaves are Curtis Flannel Cover
James River Corporation,
South Hadley, Massachusetts

Cover cloth is Iris
James River Corporation,
South Hadley, Massachusetts